AF517925

# BIRDS *of* Lucknow

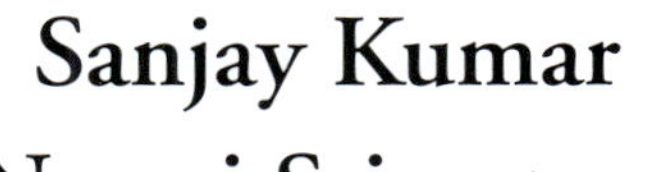

**Sanjay Kumar**
**Neeraj Srivastava**

Foreword by
**Dr Asad R Rahmani**

BLOOMSBURY
NEW DELHI • LONDON • OXFORD • NEW YORK • SYDNEY

BLOOMSBURY INDIA
Bloomsbury Publishing India Pvt. Ltd
Second Floor, LSC Building No. 4, DDA Complex, Pocket C – 6 & 7,
Vasant Kunj, New Delhi 110070

BLOOMSBURY, BLOOMSBURY INDIA and the Diana logo are
trademarks of Bloomsbury Publishing Plc

First published in 2021

Copyright © Sanjay Kumar and Neeraj Srivastava, 2021

All photographs in the book unless otherwise stated
© Sanjay Kumar and Neeraj Srivastava.

Sanjay Kumar and Neeraj Srivastava have asserted their rights under the Indian
Copyright Act to be identified as the Authors of this work

All rights reserved. No part of this publication may be reproduced or transmitted
in any form or by any means, electronic or mechanical, including photocopying,
recording or any information storage or retrieval system, without the prior
permission in writing from the publishers

This book is solely the responsibility of the author and the publisher has had
no role in the creation of the content and does not have responsibility for
anything defamatory or libellous or objectionable

Bloomsbury Publishing Plc does not have any control over, or responsibility for,
any third-party websites referred to or in this book. All internet addresses
given in this book were correct at the time of going to press.
The author and publisher regret any inconvenience caused if addresses have changed or
sites have ceased to exist, but can accept no responsibility for any such changes

ISBN: 978-93-89449-99-0
2 4 6 8 10 9 7 5 3 1

Printed and bound in India by Thomson Press India Ltd.

To find out more about our authors and books, visit
www.bloomsbury.com and sign up for our newsletters

# CONTENTS

Nikon
Nikon

The first sentence of the book, 'Birds are one of the most important indicators of the health of the ecosystem', sets the tone of this magnificently illustrated, much-awaited book by two prominent conservationists of Uttar Pradesh. They rightly point out that 'The very survival of a healthy population of birds ensures a healthy environment around us'.

Lucknow is an old city, famous for its rich cultural heritage, splendid buildings, lush gardens, meandering Gomti River, one of the largest army cantonments of India, Lucknow-*gharana* of music, *gazals* and *thumris*, and the cradle of a well known Ganga-Jamuna *tahzeeb*. Not many people know that at one time, it was famous for bird trade, both for food and pet purposes, that created its own subculture of bird trappers, bird keepers, cage makers, seed suppliers and falconers. All this gradually and rightly disappeared from the early 1970s, after the enactment of the Indian Wildlife (Protection) Act, 1972. One aspect that is still surviving is the diversity of birds in the environs of Lucknow.

Sanjay Kumar, a high-ranking IAS officer and Neeraj Srivastava, an officer in the State Transport Department, Uttar Pradesh—both amateur birdwatchers—need to be congratulated for introducing us to the wonderful world of birdlife of Lucknow. Despite the fact that Lucknow has grown from a sleepy town of 489,000 people in 1950, to a dazzling city of 3,765,700 in 2021, and despite the fact that Lucknow has lost almost all the mango orchards, it still has 360 species of birds. Many species, unfortunately, are not so common now. Nonetheless, they sometimes make an appearance to a discerning birdwatcher. This rich birdlife is mainly due to the large numbers of gardens, the Gomti River and the 5,000-acre Kulrail Reserve Forest. Along with this, we have the sprawling National Botanical Research Institute, Remote Sensing Application Centre, Residency Complex and a large cantonment that fortunately still has large avenue trees and old attractive British-era houses, surrounded by trees.

Both the authors are keen observers of Nature and equally keen photographers. The result is an eminently readable book with amazing images of birds and their habitats. The design and layout of this coffee-table book is pleasant—a bird book has to be pleasant. Isn't it? It is difficult to decide from where to start. Let us start with the cover. It shows a proud and arrogant-looking male Sunbird in its finest breeding plumage, dwarfing the fact that it is only 10 cm long. When you have confidence, size does not matter! The Sunbird is found all over Lucknow in any housing colony with bushes, shrubs and trees.

Birds are classified into families, genus and species. The book gives a brief introduction of the family, and names all the species found in Lucknow. Due to constraints of space, all species are not described in detail. For example, Family Laniidae has six species in Lucknow, but only two species (Long-tailed Shrike and Southern Grey Shrike) are described with photographs. Similarly, in Family Anatidae (ducks, geese and swans), 25 species are listed from Lucknow (including the extinct Pink-headed Duck), but only 12 species are described.

Owing to the strategic importance of Lucknow, particularly after the First War of Independence in 1857, the British established a large army base (cantonment) in Lucknow. British are curious people by nature, and this curiosity extends to natural history, particularly ornithology. The result is that we have many historical records—specimen collection, sight records and hunting records—from the Lucknow environs. The authors have briefly dwelt on the history of ornithology in the Awadh region. This is an interesting subject on its own, and I hope the authors will one day bring out a separate book on this issue.

This lovely book ends with a brief description of the major parks and gardens of Lucknow, where some species described in this book can be seen. Some of them are now totally surrounded by *vikas*, but most of the bigger ones retain their natural charm. High bird diversity is the finest example of a healthy environment. A healthy environment is a safeguard against natural and man-made disasters. It has also been proved by my scientific studies that a healthy environment increases Gross Happiness Index and helps maintain social order. One cannot have negative feelings when you see a beautiful Sunbird, or hear a Red-whiskered Bulbul singing. While I write this foreword during COVID lockdown, the only positive things I see is a flock of Jungle Babbler foraging in the garden or an Iora feeding its young ones in a leafy tree, unmindful of the fact that the humanity is behind bars.

This book reminds us that birds (and all biodiversity) are an integral part of our life. The more we respect Nature, the more bountiful she will be towards us. Birds are a small, but beautiful, link to Nature. I hope this book will make all Lucknowites proud of the natural heritage around us and, also, to the presence of two prominent citizens who created this wonderful book. Their creativity and passion for birds has brought out the flying gems, that were hidden from us all these years.

**– Dr Asad R Rahmani**

Crimson Sunbird

# PREFACE

There was a time when we used to sleep under the stars, breathe fresh air, and witness sunrise and sunset, day after day. One of the most astonishing sights that we witnessed, especially at dawn, was the movement of birds in the sky. The memory of the perfect formation and discipline of those birds in flight is still fresh in our minds. Though one might get used to such sights, one can never truly cease to be amazed by it. Being close to Nature has surely left an indelible impression on mankind.

As the primary user and beneficiary of natural resources, we humans have the responsibility to contribute towards balancing and conserving the ecosystem that we are a part of. For that, one needs to have an in-depth understanding of the natural world. Nature is heterogeneous and full of remarkable creatures, intermixed in a complex system, functioning separately or together, to maintain a sustainable atmosphere for all living beings, including us. Birds are an inseparable part of our ecosystem and also one of the most fascinating members of the natural world. They play an important role in maintaining ecological balance, and are aptly called bioindicators of the ecosystem they inhabit.

With this in mind, an effort has been made to enable the non-ornithological reader, who knows little or nothing about birds, to recognise, and hence develop an interest in some of the common species found in India, and particularly in Lucknow. This book is dedicated to those readers who derive deep, albeit simple joy, from observing the habits of the wild birdlife, but are often denied a wholesome experience by their want of knowledge of the birds concerned, their names and what is already known about them. It is also aimed that this repository of the avifaunal richness of Lucknow might allow the responsible authorities to derive useful inferences while planning a green and healthy urbanscape and waterscape subsequently, and take a prudent and sustainable approach towards nature and natural resources. This book has been written with the hope that it would help shape the landscape of rapidly developing cities in a more sustainable manner so that it is both healthy and delightful.

Locations or site names are not mentioned along with the description of bird species in the chapter 'Birds of Lucknow—A Showcase'. It is done so as to keep those long lensers at bay who, often intentionally or unintentionally to get a closer view of the bird, not only violate the conservation norms but may adversely affect the species and habitat.

Asian Koel

Indian Peacock

# WHAT ARE BIRDS?

Birds constitute a class of the vertebrate animals. They are placed higher than the reptiles as they are warm-blooded, and lower than the mammals as they do not suckle their young but lay eggs. They have neither lips nor teeth; their mouths being encased in horn and consolidated into a beak. But the most vital difference between birds and all other vertebrate animals lies in the fact that they have modified forelimbs, which function as organs of flight. The sky is their world and the trees are their home. They breathe pure air, and as they look around them on fields and hills and sky, they see beasts and men crawling on the ground beneath. The institution of the family, which is the most sacred thing in our own social system, exists among birds in its purest form. A great majority of them are monogamous during the nesting season. In fact, many pair for life and become devotedly attached to each other. Mates are won over by courtship. Birds are particularly tidy and clean when it comes to hygiene, so much so that much of their time is spent in maintenance activities to keep themselves clean. Many of them bathe regularly, while others prefer a dust bath. The male bird is generally larger and stronger, but the reverse has been observed in the case of birds of prey.

Pond Heron

Grey Wagtail

Common Tailor

# WHY DO BIRDS MATTER?

Birds are one of the most important indicators of the health of the ecosystem. Their habitat preferences and dependency on Nature makes them credible bioindicators. What we need to know is that they are the ambassadors of the natural world, that is rapidly receding from us. Fewer and fewer people are able to experience Nature in a direct, unadulterated way and birds are perhaps few of the potential mediums through which we can still connect with nature.

Birds have shorter life cycles as compared to a number of other forms of life on earth. In case of local birds of a particular region, one has access to this complete cycle. Migration of birds across long distances also allows us to observe and study a variety of species. Birds ruled the world for more than 65 million years. They were the ones that spread out and rapidly evolved to fill every conceivable ecological niche in tens of millions of years. We believe that evolution is witness to the importance of these amazing creatures and they deserve focused attention, study and respect. Birds have proven to be beneficial to us and maintain the delicate balance of nature. Habitat alteration and destruction, poaching for meat, illegal hunting for traditional medicine and capture for pet trade are the main threats to several species of birds today.

Sarus Crane

# LUCKNOW THROUGH THE PASSAGE OF TIME

The Chattar Manzil Palace and the Royal Boat of Oudh

Lucknow through Metamorphosis

The city of Lucknow was an important centre in both Awadh, and later in the United Provinces of Agra and Awadh. In 1936, Lucknow was declared the provincial capital of Uttar Pradesh and government offices were transferred from Allahabad to Lucknow. Eleven years later (in 1947), the United Provinces of Agra and Awadh formed one of the states of the Republic of India. Finally, in 1950, the entire province was given the name of Uttar Pradesh (UP). Since then, Lucknow has remained the capital of the state of Uttar Pradesh.

## Natural History

Prior to coming under the dominion of various rulers, India and this part of the country, to be specific, the entire Awadh region, was blanketed by virgin forests and thickets, that made it almost impenetrable. But as the region grew in importance, more and more of its forest cover was removed. Large tracts of natural forests were cleared and brought under the plough, until the swampy marshland of the Terai checked the destructive advances of man in the north. Much of the native vegetation suffered greatly because of rampant exploitation at the hands of timber merchants, which disturbed the ecological balance of the Terai region. Lucknow is now left with a few scattered, fragmented and small natural forests, low-lying areas alongside man-made canals and the Gomti River. However, structures with large gardens, compounds of heritage buildings decorated with large, old, native trees and aesthetic landscape are known to support varied birdlife. There are records of active wetlands within the city but now, due to negligent and so-called development, almost all of them are disappearing. In spite of these adverse conditions, there are still natural wetlands in suburban Lucknow, that support a sizable number of avifauna. These ecologically prosperous areas are home to many birds, including the Sarus crane.

## Topography

Lucknow constitutes a fraction of the flatlands in Uttar Pradesh lying diagonally across its centre. The geographical location of Lucknow is between 26°30' to 27°10' North and 80°30' to 81°13' East, at an elevation of 123 meters above the sea level. The district lies almost at the centre of the area between the Ganga River on one side, and the Ghaghra River on the other. To the north and east of the Gomti River, the land is an undulating plain and a number of rivulets, which traverse these plains, finally join the Gomti on its left bank. Lucknow is surrounded by rural towns and villages like the orchard town of Malihabad, the historic Kakori, Mohanlal Ganj, Gosainganj, Chinhat and Itaunja. On its east lies Barabanki district, west lies Unnao district, south Raebareli district and in the north lie Sitapur and Hardoi districts. The Gomti River, the chief geographical feature of Lucknow, meanders through the city, dividing it into the Trans-Gomti and Cis-Gomti regions. As mentioned in the gazetteer, Lucknow is the smallest district in point of area in Uttar Pradesh. The area of the district, on the basis of professional survey by the Survey of India works out 624,896 acres which is equivalent to 976.4 square miles, with sizeable area under verdant covers. Population as per the census of 1951 was 1,128,101 of which the rural population accounted for 607,577 which is more than 50% of total population of the district. The city has now expanded on all sides and covers 3,204 square kilometres but it did so at the cost of its natural green cover. In short, Lucknow is now substantially far from what it used to be in the past, the city of gardens.

Rumi Gate, Lucknow

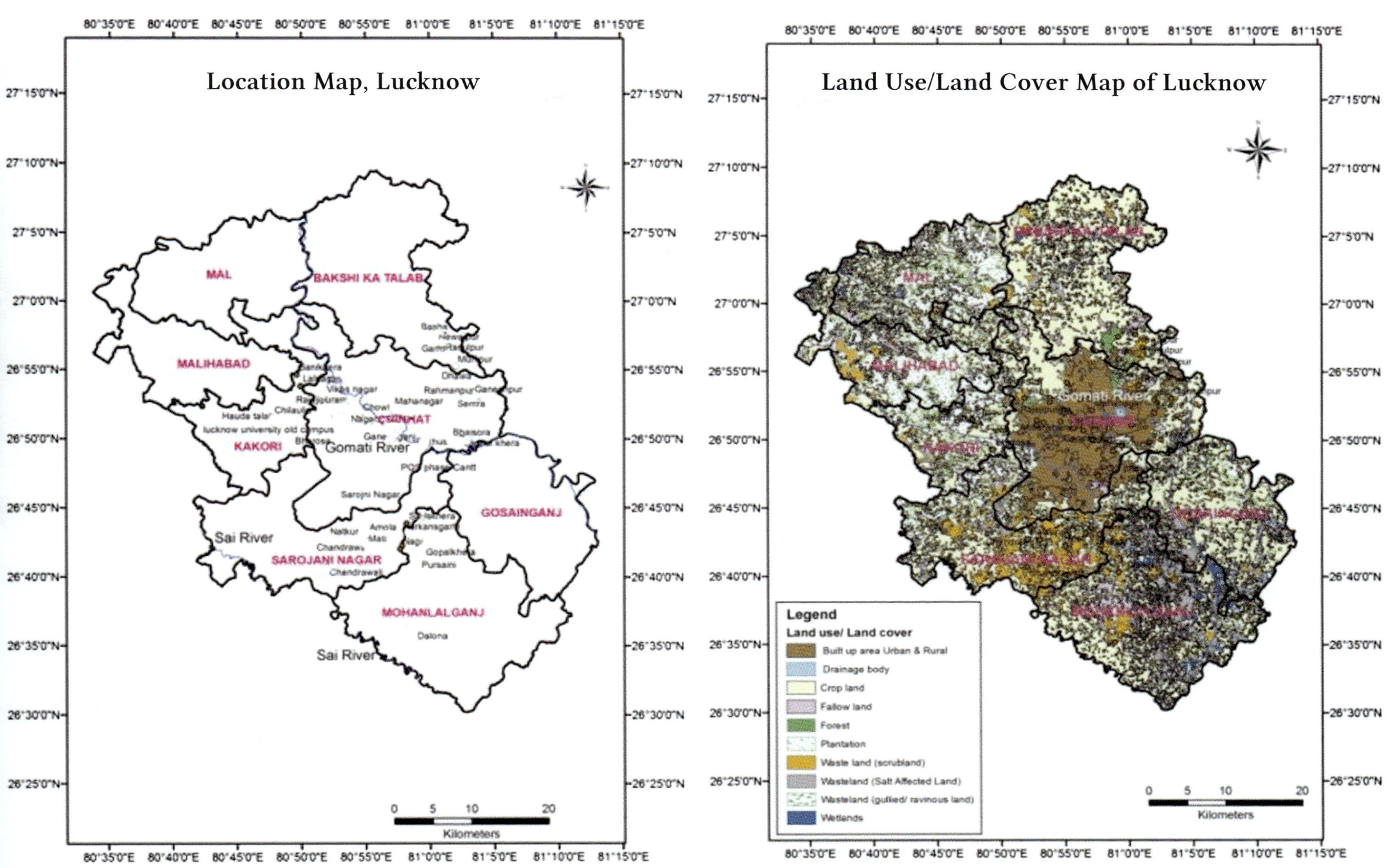


*Source:* Birbal Sahni Institute of Palaeobotany, Lucknow.

## River Gomti

The Gomti, an alluvial river of the Indo-Gangetic Plain and one of the important tributaries of the Ganga, is the only river that does not originate in the mountains, instead, it originates near Mainkot, from a lake—FulharJheel—in Madhotanda, about 30 kilometres east of Pilibhit, just adjacent to Kheri.It flows tortuously southwards through Kheri, Sitapur and Lucknow, where it bends sharply south-eastwards through Barabanki and Sultanpur, only to join the Ganga in Gazipur. The main tributaries of the Gomti in Lucknow are Akraddi, Jhilingi, Behta and Loni on the right side while Kukrail, Reth and other minor streams on the left. There are a few patches of well-wooded areas on the sides of some of the tributaries, outside the city limits.

River Gomti is an important part of the landscape of Lucknow as it also provides and supports a vital habitat for a number of waterbirds, both local and migratory species. The areas covered with reed and bushes, alongside the river, also help sustain diversity in birdlife.

River Gomti

## Landscape and Avifaunal Diversity

Lucknow is better known to the rest of the world as an important centre of culture, fine arts and traditional cuisine. Admirably, a lot has been said and written about the idiosyncrasies of the inhabitants of Lucknow. As far as birdlife of this region is concerned, not much is mentioned on it. However, a few written historical accounts are available, which describe rich landscape and exuberant birdlife of this region. Specifically the aquatic birdlife, which is mentioned extensively: waterfowl is termed as game and the hunters are called sportsmen. These sportsmen, used to hunt mainly in the winter season. Plains of Awadh, of which Lucknow was a fraction, being an important part of the fertile Gangetic plains and with numerous active wetlands, used to be a haven for waterfowls. Most observations, in this case, were recorded by the then British officials who used to be regular visitors to Awadh. These on-field observations were regularly published in journals, such as *Stray Feathers* and the *IBIS*, the two prestigious journals of those times on ornithology. These journals are still rated as among the most reliable references resources in the field of natural history. Sporadic ornithological references of Lucknow as an important part of Awadh, as a division and as a district, may be found in these periodicals. At this point, it would be appropriate and fair to introduce the readers to George or Geo Reid and William Jesse, whom we may rate as major ornithological contributors towards the knowledge regarding the diversity of birds. George Reid was an ornithologist in British India, while Jesse was a British zoologist and naturalist. Ornithological contributions by these two are by far the best and valuable references available regarding the birdlife of Lucknow. While going through their papers and field notes, the reader might be able to develop a better understanding of the landscape and birdlife of this region, then and now.

The Indian Mutiny 1857–1859

## Leaves from History

The following is the historical account that describes the topographical status of the Lucknow division (extended upto Unnao and Barabanki district):

> 'There is not much diversity in the soil. The soil is fertile and productive, forming, as it does, part of the "Garden of India". The climate of the Division is generally considered healthy, and, except in the moist and well-wooded tracts in the vicinity of the Ganges and the Gogra (the River Ghaghra), where malarious fever is common during, and for a while after the rains, differs but little from that of Lucknow itself. Explaining the region as tame, domestic and monotonous without the presence of hills or forest, yet with alternate presence of villages, flooded areas and tracts of Dhak (Butea frondosa) jungle intermixed in some places with thorny shrubs afford excellent shelter for partridges, popular game birds.'

William Jesse, much inspired by the narratives of George Reid, describes the landscape as:

> 'The general aspect of the Division is a flat cultivated plain, interspersed with jheels, mango-topes, maidans and nullahs. In some localities, there are stretches of dhak jungle, very beautiful when in full bloom, intermingled with Corounda, in which nilgai, hares, and partridges are to be found. A characteristic of Oudh is its mango-groves (*Mangifea indica*), which are so numerous that they give an appearance of the horizon being bounded by a continuous forest. These groves, being in most cases free from brushwood and undergrowth, harbour no game but afford cool retreats to man and beast in hot weather.
>
> Numerous jheels in the region are usually situated in the middle of some usar [unproductive] plain surrounded by dhak, grass, or corouuda jungle, though of late years, owing to the destruction of the brushwood, they are of a more open nature than they formerly were.
>
> The Gangetic plains, of which Lucknow is a part, was dotted with numerous productive wetlands. These sites claimed to be one of the finest areas which supported diverse species of waterfowls was a big attraction for hunters orsportsmen. 15th November to 15th February is the best time for the year for sporting community and considered as "season of the year".'[1]

George Reid emphasised much on waterbirds or waterfowls in his work. He has referred winter, especially to the sporting community, as the season of the

[1] Jesse, William. 'Birds of Lucknow Division.' *Stray Feathers*, vol. 9, 1880, p. 492.

year. The jhils are then covered with wild fowl, the marshes teem with snipe, while the woods and meadows swarm with thousands of migratory birds, many of them strikingly beautiful compared with the resident species. Describing the waterlogged areas, the most important habitat of waterfowls, he wrote,'Remarkable as it may seem, these jhils have ever since been metamorphosed in character. Some of the sub-divisions where jhils were particularly numerous are Mohanlalganj, Sehsindi, Rahimabad and Itaunja in Lucknow district. Many of them were fine expanse of water; some of them used to be covered with the lotus and other aquatic plants, other again being free from such vegetation but had, characteristically, one thing in common, plenty of waterfowl in cold weather.'

Among the earliest observations of decline in the avian population is one from Lucknow by Reid, who wrote in 1887. He speculated that the drought of 1877 was one of the causes of the decline in the population of waterbirds. He then points out that the famine following it led to an increase in *singhara* (water chestnut) cultivation in some of the wetlands. Another reason behind the decline of waterfowls was the advent of railways and outreach within these jheels. The increased presence of sportsmen and the disturbance created by gunshots further reduced their numbers. Native fowlers, in the ante-railway days, used to net thousands, many of them, rare ducks—on jheels, where they find it profitless to catch them now, birds being scarce on account of the 'potting' continually going on. All this led to a decline in the presence of water birds, and also, disappearance of bird-trappers in the market.

> 'The Crested Grebe, too, is another bird that has become exceedingly rare in localities where formerly it was abundant. Slaughtered wholesale, and systematically, for the sake of its beautiful skin, we now seldom see its silvery-white breast glistening in the sun. Slowly, but surely, too, our beautiful White Herons and Egrets are facing a similar fate. A price has been put upon their feathery snow-white plumes, and man must need debase his manhood by pandering to the insatiable vagaries or depravities of fashion.
>
> If I have written strongly, it is because I feel strongly on a subject that requires immediate attention. The destruction not only of Grebe, Herons, Egrets and Pheasants but of beautiful birds of every variety, is going on apace, and while the depredators are reaping a rich harvest by pilfering the nation's property—its game birds and the beautiful songsters—those who ought to protect them, by holding aloof, are simply participating in their destruction. This state of affairs will only lead to an extermination of various species, when, of course, everyone will regret the result, but then, who would have thought of preventing it?'

Reid published a catalogue of the birds of the Lucknow Museum in 1889. George Reid died on 16 March 1901. The story of Lucknow's declining bird population did not stop there. In 1902, William Jesse, at the La Martiniere College, received most of Reid's notes and he, thereafter, began writing on the continued decline.

There are sporadic references to some of the rare birds in this region in various historical works. In Volume VIII of *Stray Feathers* (1879), Geo Reid wrote about the presence of two pink-headed ducks (*Rhodonessa caryophyllacea*) in a pond at Rahimabad, some 25 miles away from Lucknow. There is a mention of another specimen of the same bird at the Lucknow Museum.This bird was also reported in Lucknow in the *2001 Annual Report of BirdLife International.*

Other references that may be of interest are:

1. One specimen of the lesser White-fronted goose (*Anser erythropus*) was procured by Dr Bonavia near Lucknow (Hume, AO, *Stray Feathers*, 1879).
2. There is one undated record of Baikal teal (*Annas formosa*) from Lucknow (George Reid, 1881).
3. A specimen of Marbled teal (*Marmaronetta angustirostris*) was captured and given to Lucknow Museum by a wildfowler (Reid, 1881).
4. A fine male common Goldeneye (*Bucephala clangula*) was caught by fowlers near Lucknow around 1870 (Stuart Baker, 1921).

Lucknow through the Passage of Time

# SPORTING ASSOCIATION WITH BIRDS

Lucknow was, once upon a time, a city accredited with a different sort of amusement worldwide. It was during the reign of Nawabs, who enjoyed the company of big mammals and birds in a different way. Organising fights between beasts of prey, bird-fighting and bird-flying were the kind of sports adopted by different classes in Lucknow. Fights between predators were confined to the royal court as keeping the large animals, training them and organising grand fests for the fights, was all beyond the means of even the richest man. This practice came to an end with the end of the royal court in Lucknow. But bird-fighting was much more affordable. Any interested person, even from the common class, could keep and train a quail, cock or any other bird. Birds that people in Lucknow used for bird-fighting were cocks, bush quails, partridges, lavwey, guldums (bulbuls), lals (munias), pigeons and parrots. The Lucknow pigeon-flying and quail-fighting were famous throughout the country. The degree of perfection to which the admirers of the game raised them was no less than a work of fine art. Keeping and caring for them as pets has a plethora of interesting account.

## Cock Fighting

Asil, as it is commonly known, is a thoroughbred cock which was considered to be the best fighter, apart from other breeds of cock. Braver than a tiger, as quoted, they would sooner die than turn away from a fight.[1] Experts believe the breed had originated in Arabia. Interest in cock fighting dates back to the time of Nawab Shuja-ud-Daula, who was extremely fond of the sport. General Martin, also a great lover of the game, participated with the Nawab. The Nawab used to bet his cocks against those of the general public. During the breaks between the fights (called *pani* or water), birds were removed from the arena by their respective parties. Their wounds were cleaned and water was poured on their heads to revitalise them. Also, before preparing the cocks for the fight, a round of massage of bird's limb, sprinkled with water, tending to their beak and claws, were an essential part of the sport.

## Quail Fighting

The interest of quail fighting came to Lucknow from Punjab. It is said that during the time of Sadat Ali Khan, some gypsies brought the bush quail with them. There are two types of quails: the bush quail and the button quail. The bush quail is found in Punjab, which is bigger and stronger then button quail. In Lucknow, both types of quails were found. However, the button quail, owing to its smaller size and status as a powerful fighter, was considered more suitable for fighting. Quail-fighting was easy to organise because space was never an issue. It was often organised indoors, hence the whole family, including women, could watch the fight. For this reason, the sport became extremely popular in Lucknow. Dainty bamboo cages adorned with strips of ivory were made to keep the birds.

## Partridge Fighting

Partridges had never been an attraction for the sport for the upper class or noblemen, while villagers and people from the 'lower classes' showed great interest in them. It was a different game altogether. Partridges, when fighting, leap into the air more than other birds. The birds were trained by rolling them in dust and making them race. Termites were used to excite and work them up.

## Lavwa Fighting

Lavwa is a variety of partridge, smaller than a quail. While the other birds fought over grain, they fought over a female. The sport was more popular in the state of Rewa and other regions of Central India, but people in Lucknow too followed it to a certain extent. Lavwa fighting began before quail fighting, but eventually the latter became more prevalent and the former died out.

## Guldum Fighting

Guldums or rose-tails, or bulbuls as they are known now, were trained by sprinkling grains before them. When they fought, both the birds flew into the air and as they closed in on each other, became enmeshed and then descended still entangled. It was a sport that was more popular in villages and among the lower classes while the upper classes never showed much interest in this sport.

## Pigeons and Parrots

Pigeons can be classed among those tame species of birds in which human beings have taken interest from the ancient times. Among various varieties, tumbler pigeons were most popular. They were first brought to Lucknow from Kabul and was the first variety to be flown. Tumbler pigeons only fly in flocks. As per an interesting account, pigeon-flying reached such perfection in Delhi that it is said that when the last Mughal Emperor, Bahadur Shah, went out in a procession, a flock of 200 pigeons would fly above his head to shade him from the sun.

In Lucknow, one of the nawabs, Wazid Ali Shah was extremely fond of pigeons and possessed a huge collection of the birds. When he died, he had more than 24,000 pigeons, with hundreds of keepers to look after them.

[1] Sharar, Abdul Halim, et al. *Lucknow: The Last Phase of an Oriental Culture*. Oxford University Press, 1975.

**Disclaimer:** Descriptions, at some places, may look exaggerated or seem to eulogise the then Nawabs. Please note that the authors do not support such anecdotes and these have been included only to make an interesting read.

*Source:* Poster Print of Colonel Mordaunt Watching a Cock Fight at Lucknow, India, 1790. *Artist:* Johan Zoffany

# HOW TO USE THIS BOOK

The book begins with customary but vital referential inputs about topography and natural history of birds of Lucknow. A short write up on association of birds with different perspective, unveils the ways of lifestyle used for amusement of people of Lucknow, both common and royals.

The narratives on cognition and intelligence are particularly informative and give a glimpse into the rich and diversified interest in the birds and their habitat. A glossary of critical ornithological terms and abbreviations are given to ease the process of reading the book.

*Birds of Lucknow* is divided in 52 chapters. '*Birds of Lucknow—A Showcase*' is the main and biggest chapter of this book. All bird species are arranged in their family groups, starting from Phasianidae (Galliformes) and ending with Emberizidae (Passeriformes or perching birds). To know about the bird and the family it belongs, Birds are placed categorically and collectively in the family group they represent. As per the check list, Birds belong to a total of 65 family groups. A pictures of habitat or site of each family with brief description of each of the family group is given, supplemented by a habitat photograph. It is to understand the respective bird better. In the following pages, brief descriptions of the species, its category and global status [as per the assessment of International Union for Conservation of nature (IUCN)] is accompanied by photographs of the species discussed. These descriptive images would help our readers to have a fairly clear idea about the bird's plumage, habit and preferences. Seasonal status of bird in this region, Global status and standard size of the bird are given with each photograph, a size scale is also placed alongside each image. It would help to have a practical size estimate by looking at the position of dot between the model bird species.

## Size Scale

Name and size of some of most common or familiar birds are given. This has been replicated on each page where a bird species is displayed. A dot (•) is placed in between the species shown above to assess the size of the respective bird. This is to facilitate the reader to have a fair idea of a bird's size.

Sarus Crane
150 cm

Black Kite
64 cm

House Crow
40 cm

Common Mynah
25 cm

House Sparrow
15 cm

## Category and Global Status

| CATEGORY | GLOBAL STATUS (as per IUCN standards) |
|---|---|
| CR = Common Resident | NE = Not Evaluated |
| CW = Common Winter Visitor | DD = Data Deficient |
| CS = Common Summer Visitor | LC = Least Concern |
| LCW = Local Common Winter Visitor | NT = Near Threatened |
| LCS = Local Common Summer Visitor | VU = Vulnerable |
| NCW = Not Common Winter Visitor | EN = Endangered |
| NCS = Not Common Summer Visitor | CR = Critically Endangered |
| SO = Stray Occurance | EW = Extinct in Wild |
| | EX = Extinct |

## Glossary

| | |
|---|---|
| Aberrant | abnormal or unusual |
| Aigrette | a bunch of the long, white, showy plumes of the egret |
| Arboreal | living in trees, especially in upper branches |
| Barred | having horizontal bands (as on tail, wings) |
| Canopy | leafy foliage of treetops |
| Casque | a hard enlargement on upper mandible of hornbills |
| Crepuscular | active at dusk (twilight) and dawn |
| Crest | extended feathers on head |
| Crown | upper part of head |
| Culmen | the ridge of the upper mandible |
| Deciduous | trees that shed their leaves annually |
| Diurnal | active during day time |
| Epicarp | the outermost layer of the pericarp |
| Flight feathers | the primaries, secondaries and tail feathers |
| Gape | the mouth and the fleshy corner of the bill, which can extend back below the eyes |
| Graduated tail | a tail in which the longest feathers are the central pair and the shortest the outermost, with those in between intermediate in length |
| Gregarious | living in flocks or in communities |
| Gular pouch | a loose and pronounced area of skin extending from the throat (e.g., on hornbills) |
| Mandible | the lower or upper half of the bill |
| Morph | a distinct plumage type that may occur in the same species |
| Nape | hind-neck or nuchal area, back of neck |
| Passerines | a perching bird |
| Raptor | a bird of prey or a predatory bird (eagle, hawks, buzzards) |
| Rufous | reddish brown |
| Terrestrial | living or occurring mainly on the ground |
| Vent | the area around the cloaca (anal opening), just behind the legs |
| Wattle | a lore of bare, often brightly coloured skin attached to the head (at the bill base, most frequently) |
| Wing-bar | generally, a narrow and well-defined dark or pale bar across head or upper wing |

A Showcase

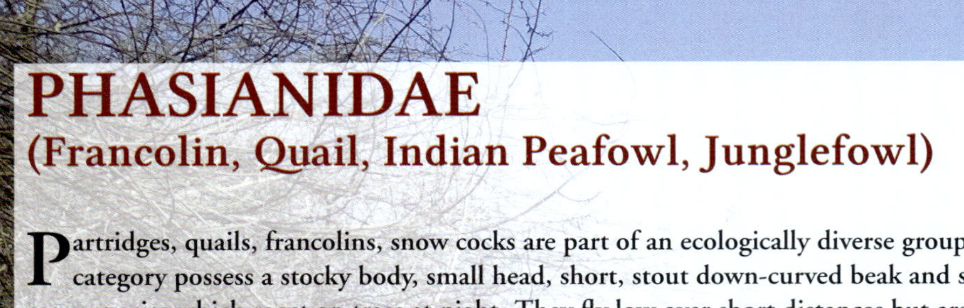

# PHASIANIDAE
## (Francolin, Quail, Indian Peafowl, Junglefowl)

Partridges, quails, francolins, snow cocks are part of an ecologically diverse group of birds with a worldwide distribution, excluding the polar regions. Birds in this category possess a stocky body, small head, short, stout down-curved beak and strong legs. They are mostly terrestrial, feeding and nesting on the ground, except for some species which roost on trees at night. They fly low over short distances but are good runners; often prefer to trust their feet rather than wings. They like to feed on seeds, fruits, buds, roots and leaves, besides invertebrates. The city of Lucknow, as per historical records, used to have many species of francolins and quails, then referred to as game birds. Most of these species are still surviving in the city and can be located in the green expanse around many monumental heritage sites, and also within the scrub vegetation on the outskirts of the city.

- Black Francolin
- Grey Francolin
- Common Quail
- Rain Quail
- King Quail
- Jungle Bush Quail
- Red Junglefowl
- Indian Peafowl

## Black Francolin

*Francolinus francolinus* काला तीतर

Commonly known as kala teetar, the Black francolin or Black partridge prefers to live within thick vegetation near water. It is a secretive and shy bird, and hence not easily noticeable. Sporadic sightings have been reported from light forests in the suburb.

± 34 CM, WELL-WATERED TRACTS WITH TALL GRASS

**LCR** LC

## Grey Francolin

*Francolinus pondicerianus* सफ़ेद तीतर

Also known as the Grey partridge, the Grey francolin is a small ground bird with an orangish face and fine barring throughout. It inhabits open cultivated land or scrub jungle. In Lucknow, the bird is considered to be a game bird, and has long been domesticated and trained for bird-fighting. The bird is commonly spotted in the scrub areas in the periphery of the city.

± 32 CM, DRY LIGHT JUNGLES, AREAS WITH LOW GRASS COVER

**LCR** LC

# Red Junglefowl

*Gallus gallus* लाल जंगली मुर्ग

± 45 CM (F) TO 75 CM (M), SCRUBLANDS, SECONDARY FORESTS, FOREST EDGES

LCR | LC

The Red junglefowl is a wildfowl and said to be the ancestor of the domestic fowl. Widespread throughout South and Southeast Asia, where the fowl is generally found in mixed deciduous forests or scrub jungles interspersed with patches of cultivation. It sports lavish and brilliant hues. Owing to its preference of forested areas, it is considered to be a bioindicator of this habitat.

# Indian Peafowl

*Pavo cristatus* मोर, मयूर

± 95 CM (F), 210 CM (M), OPEN FORESTS, URBAN GARDENS, LARGE BUNGALOW PREMISES

LCR | LC

The Indian peafowl is one of the largest and most familiar ground birds. It is also our national bird. The male bird is called peacock while the female peahen. One may come across the bird in the large compounds of palatial heritage buildings, adorned with old and large trees. In Lucknow, the National Botanical Research Institute is incomparably the best place to watch and observe the enchanting activities of this bird.

# Jungle Bush Quail

## *Perdicula asiatica* जंगली लवा

A small, plump terrestrial bird, roughly spherical in shape, the Jungle Bush quail is identified by its rusty throat and rusty-and-white eyebrow. It often appears in groups in dry stony scrub jungles and dry grasslands. Generally secretive until flushed, it suddenly bursts into flight, flying low over the ground with weak whirring wing beats. It feeds on grass, seeds and small insects.

© Sunil Kini

± 17 CM, DECIDUOUS FORESTS, SCRUBLANDS AND STONY GROUNDS

LCR | LC

# Rain QuaiL

## *Coturnix coromandelica* चीना बटेर

A small-sized quail, mostly terrestrial, the Rain quail is mainly found in grassland and is more often heard than seen, especially during the months of monsoon. The male has a very distinctive and unmistakable 'whit-whit' call, repeated every few seconds, both in the morning and in the evening. This quail feeds on seeds of grasses and other plants, insect larvae and small invertebrates.

© Rajesh Panwar

± 18 CM, FARMLANDS, GRASSLANDS AND SCRUB JUNGLES

LCR | LC

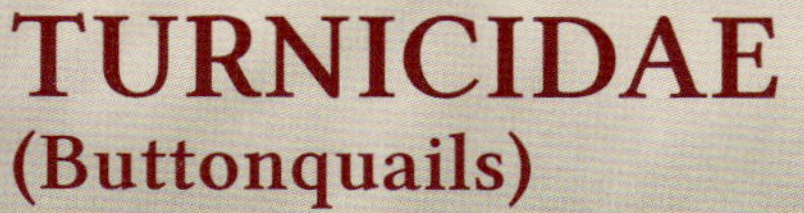

# TURNICIDAE
## (Buttonquails)

Buttonquails are small, plump terrestrial birds. They have a small head, short neck and legs and almost no tail. Found in a wide variety of habitats, mostly with low ground cover under which they readily walk or run. They are highly secretive and avoid flying until they sense danger. They feed primarily on grass and weed seeds besides small insects, picking food from the ground surface, or scratching with their feet.

# Barred Buttonquail

*Turnix suscitator* धारिया गुलू

The Barred buttonquail is a tiny quail with chin, throat and breast closely barred with black, found in scrub and grassland. Mostly terrestrial, it feeds on grass, weed, seeds, invertebrates and green shoots. Occasionally seen in the countryside, it usually moves alone or in small groups and forages among grass and leaf litter.

± 15 CM, FARMLANDS, GRASSLANDS AND SCRUBLANDS

**LCR** LC

- Small Buttonquail
- Yellow-legged Buttonquail
- Barred Buttonquail

# ANATIDAE (Ducks, Swan and Geese)

Waterbirds, popularly known as waterfowls, include classes of birds which spend most of their lives in or around water. Mostly web-footed, these birds are efficient swimmers and fully adapted for life on, or near water, floating on the water surface, and in some cases diving in, at least, shallow water. All these birds share a modified bill and tongue that can suck water through the tip and expel it from the sides. Highly gregarious in character, they can be observed feeding, roosting and resting together, often in mixed flocks. They forage by diving in the water, by surface feeding or dabbling and grazing. In Lucknow, fairly good numbers of species of water birds are migratory and stay only during winter. Out of the 36 species countrywide, 27 species are reported in this region. Among these, seven species of waterfowl were once found in the area a long time back but have not been reported in recent times. These are Greater White-fronted goose, Lesser White-fronted goose, Pink-headed duck, Baikal teal, Common goldeneye, Goosander or Common merganser and Greater scaup.

- Lesser Whistling Duck
- Greylag Goose
- Greater White-fronted Goose
- Lesser White-fronted Goose
- Bar-headed Goose
- Comb or Knob-billed Duck
- Ruddy Shelduck
- Cotton Pygmy-goose or Cotton Teal
- Gadwall
- Eurasian Wigeon
- Mallard
- Indian Spot-billed Duck
- Northern Shoveler
- Northern Pintail
- Garganey
- Baikal Teal
- Common Teal
- Red-crested Pochard
- Common Pochard
- Ferruginous Duck
- Tufted Duck
- Greater Scaup
- Common Goldeneye
- Goosander or Common Merganser
- Pink-headed Duck (Extinct)

# Bar-headed Goose

*Anser indicus* सरपट्टी सवन

± 75 CM, OPEN SANDBARS OF LARGE RIVERS, LAKES AND WETLANDS

CW | LC

One of the most striking and distinctive geese, the Bar-headed goose is claimed to be one of the world's highest-flying birds. This amazing bird migrates over the Himalayas, the highest mountain range on the planet. Its lungs are larger than other birds, which allows them to breathe efficiently in low oxygen conditions. The bird's name comes from its white head marked by two black crossbars. In winter, it dominates the avian population in wetlands and cultivated fields. Like other geese, it is quite a gregarious bird, and the flocks are sometimes very large.

# Greylag Goose

± 85 CM, OPEN SANDBARS OF LARGE RIVERS, LAKES AND WETLANDS

CW | LC

*Anser anser* स्लेटी सवन

One of the largest and bulkiest of geese, the Greylag goose is the only common goose in India besides the Bar-headed goose and, just like the latter, is only winter guest in India. Usually found in large groups in shallow wetlands, it keeps more on the shore than in the water. It can walk well and is also a fast swimmer, diving freely in play or when wounded, but cannot stay under long. It is claimed to be the first bird domesticated by humans, some 3,000 years ago, in ancient Egypt.

# Ruddy Shelduck

*Tadorna ferruginea* सुर्खाब

± 65 CM, OPEN SANDBARS OF LARGE RIVERS, LAKES AND WETLANDS

CW | LC

This showy, inedible bird, so conspicuous in its foxy-red plumage on land or water, is a bird that is hard to miss. Ruddy shelduck is a fairly large and beautiful looking duck. It attracts the onlooker's attention with its trumpeting and honking calls, especially when in flocks. It is a winter visitor in the plains, but breeds in the Himalayas and Tibet, and up to Mongolia.

# Northern Pintail

## *Anas acuta* सीन्खपर बतख

One of the most handsome and popular of the ducks, the Pintail derives its popular name from its long, pointed middle tail feathers. These are almost 9 inches long when he is in full dress. The long tail 'pins' start appearing from January onwards and fully develop by February–March, when they return home to breed. The bird migrates from its breeding grounds in the northern part of the range to spend the winter in India. It stays in wetlands in large flocks mixed with other water birds. It is migratory to this region.

± 55 CM, SHALLOW STRETCHES OF LAKES AND WETLANDS

CW | LC

# Garganey

## *Anas querquedula* चेता बतख

Often called the Blue-winged teal, the Garganey is one of the earliest winter visitors to our country. In disposition and style of flight, it is decidedly different from other ducks. Noted ornithologist, ECS Baker calls the bird's characteristic distinctive from other birds. It swims and walks as well as the common teal and dives much better. This gregarious waterfowl is also one of the most widespread waterbirds and is often seen upending and waddling on squelchy ground.

± 42 CM, SHALLOW STRETCHES OF LAKES AND WETLANDS

LCW | LC

# Mallard

± 60 CM, FRESHWATER MARSHES AND REED-EDGED LAKES

LCW LC

*Anas platyrhynchos* नीलसर बतख

Globally, the Mallard is still one of the most abundant ducks. Little needs to be said about the male mallard's plumage: lovely green head, white collar, chocolate breast, curled black tail and splendid wing-bar of blue and white. It can be seen foraging for food in water, dabbling, upending, rarely by diving; and on land, grazing, plucking seeds, grubbing for roots. It visits Lucknow only in winter.

# Red-crested Pochard

*Netta rufina* लालसिर बतख

Red-crested pochard is one of the most common and widespread migratory ducks. The big red bill and bushy chestnut head of the adult male pochard can be easily spotted from afar. In size, it is the biggest of all the diving ducks except the goosander. Usually found in well-watered wetlands, this highly gregarious bird feeds chiefly by diving, upending and head dipping to get stems, roots and seeds of aquatic vegetation.

± 55 CM, LAKES AND LARGE RIVERS

LCW | LC

# Common Pochard

*Aythya ferina* छोटी लालसिर बतख

The Common pochard is a medium-sized diving duck. The pochard is as well known a bird in India as in Europe, but only as a winter visitor. The bird is, in winter months, a common sight in marshy and reed-fringed lakes and open reservoirs. Its breeding habitat consists of wetlands in most of temperate and northern Europe. Gregarious by nature, the Common pochard often associates with winter flocks of other pochards.

© Amit Mishra

± 48 CM, LAKES, RESERVOIRS AND LARGE RIVERS

LCW | LC

# Cotton Teal or Cotton Pygmy-goose

*Nettapus coromandelianus* गिर्री बतख

The jolly little Cotton teal, smallest of the Indian ducks, is no larger than a pigeon. In old written accounts, it is also called the Goose teal by ornithologists. It frequents small patches of water as well as large water bodies. The Cotton teal can be seen nesting in the rains season, usually in hollows of mango or other trees, at a distance from water. A common bird of the wetlands, it stays within small groups and feeds on aquatic vegetation and small animals.

± 35 CM, PONDS AND TANKS, PREFERABLY THOSE COVERED WITH REEDS AND VEGETATION

CR LC

# Common Teal

*Anas crecca* छोटी मुर्गाबी

Known as Eurasian teal or Green-winged teal, the Common teal, the smallest, and one of the most handsome and sociable of Indian migratory ducks, can be at once distinguished from the rest by the brilliant patch of metallic emerald green on its wings. It migrates to Lucknow in winter and is commonly found in wetlands where it feeds on seeds and aquatic invertebrates.

± 35 CM, WETLANDS COVERED WITH VEGETATION

CW LC

## Comb Duck or Knob-billed Duck

*Sarkidiornis melanotos* नकटा

The Comb duck is a large duck and common throughout the country. Apart from its size, a large, round noticeable mound on the upper mandible makes it easy to identify in the wild. This knob is present only in the male. As the monsoon approaches, each pair selects a nesting site, usually in a tree near water or in the reeds and rushes along the wetland, where the suitable tree site is not available. They are usually found in pairs, except before the breeding season, when they form large groups.

± 70 CM, POOLS IN WELL-WOODED AREAS AND WETLANDS

LCR | LC

## Spot-billed Duck or Indian Spot-billed Duck

*Anas poecilorhyncha* गुगरल बतख

The Indian Spot-billed duck is a widespread resident bird. It prefers wetlands in the open country and feeds by dabbling for plant food, mainly in the evening or at night. Not as sociable as the other members of this group, it does not like mixing with other birds. It can be seen in small groups on shallow tracts of a waterbody. Though it prefers limiting its movement within a specific area, like all birds which are dependent on waterbodies for food, it is forced to shift its quarters in order to secure favourable conditions.

± 60 CM, WETLANDS COVERED WITH VEGETATION

LCR | LC

# PICIDAE (Woodpeckers)

Woodpeckers are medium-sized birds found both in wild and urban areas, with an adequate cover of large trees to provide them suitable nesting sites. Woodpeckers are mostly arboreal, they escavate holes on large trees to nest, hence known as cavity nesters. Their short legs, strong feet and stiff tail feathers meant for clinging to and climbing up vertical trunks and lateral branches help them forage for food. They primarily feed on ants, termites and pupae of wood-boring beetles. Many species in the family are known for their characteristic loud drumming calls. In Lucknow, bird lovers can find them in the premises of heritage sites with lush green vistas and native trees.

- Eurasian Wryneck
- Brown-capped Pygmy Woodpecker
- Yellow-crowned Woodpecker
- Lesser Yellownape
- Grey-headed Woodpecker
- Himalayan Goldenback/Flameback
- Lesser Goldenback or Black-rumped Flameback
- White-naped Woodpecker
- Streak-throated Woodpecker

# Grey-headed Woodpecker

± 32 CM, COUNTRYSIDE, BROADLEAVED FORESTS

**LCR** LC

*Picus canus* स्लेटी सिर कठ्फोड़ा

The Grey-headed woodpecker occupies a range of forest habitats as well as orchards and gardens. Also known as the Grey-faced woodpecker, it prefers areas with dead trees, to feed primarily on ants and termites besides vegetable matter, such as berries and fruits. Usually solitary, it often feeds on the ground.

# Lesser Goldenback or Black-rumped Flameback

*Dinopium benghalense* कालपुठ अंगारा कठ्फोड़ा

± 28 CM, LIGHT OR OPEN FORESTS, PARKS, GARDENS WITH OPEN TREE COVER

CR | LC

The Lesser goldenback is one of the best-known woodpecker species and quite common in Lucknow. It avoids forest areas and prefers open, cultivated districts and gardens where avenues of ancient trees provide it with a happy hunting ground. It moves around alone or in pairs, busily climbing about the trunks and branches of the trees. It virtually never perches on a twig or branch crossways. The wood-boring larvae of beetles and tree-living termites are a part of its diet. A major portion of its food consists of ants which are easily obtained, mostly on tree trunks. Though occasionally, the bird descends to the ground to procure them.

# CAPITONIDAE
## (Barbets)

Barbets are brightly coloured birds with a big head and short, heavy tail. They are named after the bristles at the base of their stout, sharp bill. Vociferously vocal birds, barbets are birds that are more often heard than seen, therefore it is difficult to locate them, especially when they are silent. Out of the 11 species found throughout the country, two species of barbets are commonly seen in Lucknow. They usually nest in holes dug high up in old, large native trees. Barbets are mainly fruit-eaters, but their fast-growing chicks are fed on a high protein diet of insects. Barbets play an important role in seed dispersal. They can be seen and heard in Lucknow throughout most of the year, except during harsh winters.

- Brown-headed Barbet
- Coppersmith Barbet

# Brown-headed Barbet

*Megalaima zeylanica* बड़ा बसन्था

± 26 CM, URBAN FORESTS, PARKS PREFERABLY WITH BROADLEAVED TREESCAPE

CR LC

The presence of the bird is revealed by its call, one of the familiar sounds in the Indian plains. This is exceedingly well-known, even people who do not know it by sight, know it by sound. A purely arboreal bird, it prefers richly-wooded and well-watered localities. The Brown-headed barbet feeds chiefly on the fruit of wild fig trees, such as the banyan and peepul. It lives high above the ground amongst heavy foliage, making it hard to spot them easily as their green plumage blends with the leaves, and the curious flesh-coloured beak and yellow eye-patch look like berries.

# Coppersmith Barbet

± 17 CM, OPEN FORESTS, PARKS, GARDENS, GROVES

CR LC

## *Megalaima haemacephala* ठठेरा बसन्था

The Coppersmith or Crimson-breasted barbet is another of those Indian birds whose voice is more familiar to most people than its appearance. It is found in the countryside where large trees abound, and is purely arboreal, sitting and feeding amongst the green leaves, and never descending either to bushes or the ground. Its green plumage allows it to easily blend into its surroundings. The bird is named after its call which has been likened to the sound of a coppersmith striking metal with a hammer. Mainly frugivores or fruit-eating, it also relishes on insects, especially winged termites. They compete with other cavity-nesting birds. It is a common bird in the city's gardens.

# BUCEROTIDAE
## (Hornbills)

Hornbills, as the name suggests, are named after a horn-like projection called a casque on their large beaks. They are fairly large birds, known for their love for berries and fruits, fig being the favourite. They swallow the whole fruit and spit out the seed intact. Hornbills fly over long distances looking for fruits. In this process of consuming fruits and spitting out countless seeds, some of the seeds find suitable conditions to grow. By carrying out the dispersal of seeds, hornbills perform the noble task of planting trees. They nest in existing holes or crevices, either in trees or rocks. The female seals herself up inside the cavity and then proceeds to moult all her flight feathers in one go while she is incubating the eggs. India boasts of nine species of hornbills and Lucknow is home to two of them.

- Indian Grey Hornbill
- Oriental Pied Hornbill

# Indian Grey Hornbill

## *Ocyceros birostris* स्लेटी धनेश

The Indian Grey hornbill is one of the most common and familiar birds of the plains. An entirely arboreal species, it rarely descends to the ground, except to pick up fallen fruits or mud pellets to seal the nest cavity during the nesting period. It can be found around old trees in large gardens, in cities and also in the countryside, but it avoids thick forests. They fly in small parties from bough to bough, eating various species of wild figs, and other fruits and seeds, green leaves, and insects. The call of the bird is a harsh squeal, distinctly reminiscent that of the common kite.

An all-season bird of Lucknow, the Indian Grey hornbill can be spotted in large compounds of palatial buildings with plenty of large, old ficus trees.

± 50 CM, OPEN FOREST, WOODED AREAS WITH FRUITING TREES

**CR** | LC

# Oriental Pied Hornbill

## *Anthracoceros albirostris* पूर्वी अबलक धनेश

Not as common as its grey cousin, the Oriental Pied hornbill has a very noisy call with squeals and chuckles, mostly a cackling 'kek-kek-kek'. This hornbill's diet consists of wild fruits, such as figs, and a diverse range of other fruits to ensure that its nutritional requirements are met. It is regarded as one of the most important agents of seed dispersal.

± 57 CM, OPEN FORESTS, GROVES AND LARGE FRUIT TREES

**LCR** | LC

# UPUPIDAE

## Hoopoe: Common Hoopoe

*Upupa epops* हुदहुद

An attractive bird with fawn-coloured plumage and a noticeable crown of feathers, hoopoe loves to inhabit a neighbourhood with groves of trees, thin scrub-forest and the outskirts of villages, where it frequents mud walls and deserted or ruined buildings. It spends most of its time in the company of other ground-foraging birds, probing the roots of grass and the interstices of the soil or turning over leaves and rubbish for insects, caterpillars and grubs. It walks with great ease and methodically quarters the ground. While feeding, the crest is depressed and closed, but it invariably erects it for a second on settling after a flight. Unlike most other birds, the hoopoe doesn't gather twigs to make a nest, rather it looks for holes in tree trunks, cliffs and walls (in urban environments).

± 30 CM, OPEN COUNTRY, CULTIVATION

**CR** LC

# CORACIIDAE (Rollers)

- Indian Roller
- European Roller

Stocky, big-headed and brightly plumaged birds of open habitats, rollers are usually seen perched on overhead telegraphic wires or other exposed perches, preferably by an agricultural field. They feed largely on insects and play an important role in controlling the population of harmful insects. India is home to only two species of rollers and both of them are found in Lucknow. Indian roller is the local common variety, while European roller is the passing migrant species.

# Indian Roller

± 32 CM, OPEN WOODLANDS, CULTIVATION, GROVES AND GARDENS

CR | LC

## *Coracias benghalensis* देसी नीलकंठ

The Indian roller is a brightly coloured bird with various shades of blue on its wings, tails and belly, that are often more prominent when the bird is in flight. Generally, it sits on any convenient perch and waits patiently until some desirable prey comes into sight; then it swoops down to grab it and returns to its perch. Poetically described as 'a lovely bird with azure wings', this bird is an ornament to any landscape. The Indian roller is also extremely useful as it feeds mostly on large insects, such as grasshoppers, crickets and beetles, and occasionally on small mice, frogs and snakes. It is commonly found in and around Lucknow.

## European Roller

± 31 CM, OPEN WOODLANDS AND CULTIVATION

CR LC

*Coracias garrulus* विलायती नीलकंठ

The European roller is similar but a bit paler to its Indian cousin, both in appearance and habits, though not as common in Lucknow. This bird is just as spectacular and distinctive—overall brilliant blue, with rusty back, stout crow-like bill. It favours countrysides and suburbs with scattered trees and wooded patches. Its food mostly consists of large insects, such as grasshoppers. It can be seen perched, either alone or in small groups, on bare snags, wires and other prominent perches, and also on the ground.

# ALCEDINIDAE, HALCYONIDAE, CERYLIDAE (Kingfishers)

Kingfishers are widely distributed birds. They are brightly coloured, chunky and have a conspicuously large head and short legs. Although it is commonly believed that kingfishers mainly live near rivers and feed only on fish, many species live away from water and eat small invertebrates. They consume a wide range of prey, usually caught by swooping down from a perch. Most kingfishers feed on fish, which they catch by diving into the water headfirst. Like other members of their order, they nest in cavities, usually tunnels, dug into natural or artificial banks in the ground. Kingfishers are, generally, solitary birds.

- Common Kingfisher
- Stork-billed kingfisher
- White-throated Kingfisher
- Pied Kingfisher

# White-throated Kingfisher

*Halcyon smyrnensis* सफ़ेद छाती किलकिला

± 27 CM, FORESTS, CULTIVATION, WATER POOLS, SLOW-MOVING STREAMS, CANALS

**CR** LC

Widely distributed throughout the country, the White-throated kingfisher is one of the most characteristic birds of the plains. While the other kingfishers described in this work are purely waterbirds, living chiefly on fish, this variety of kingfisher is mainly a land bird and feeds largely on insects, lizards, frogs and the like. It captures its prey by sweeping down on them from an elevated perch. It has been observed that this bird plunges into the water to catch a fish, and also dives after freshwater crabs, which it beats to a pulp before swallowing. It is commonly found in Lucknow.

# Stork-billed Kingfisher

*Pelargopsis capensis* बड़चोंच किलकिला

± 35 CM, SHADY AREAS IN FORESTS WITHIN THE VICINITY OF WATER, SLOW-MOVING STREAMS

NCR | LC

Largest among all kingfishers found in Lucknow, the Stork-billed kingfisher prefers to perch quietly whilst seeking food. It is a very territorial bird. Predominantly a fish-eater, it also hunts frogs, crabs, rodents and even young birds. The Stork-billed kingfisher occasionally makes an appearance in Lucknow.

## Common Kingfisher

*Alcedo atthis* छोटी किलकिली

Also known as the Eurasian kingfisher or the River kingfisher, the Common kingfisher is a sparrow-sized bird and well known as a waterbird, frequenting freshwater of every description. This kingfisher usually captures its food by plunging obliquely into the water from an overhanging bough, stump or clump of reeds, or a similar vantage point on which it sits motionless waiting for something to come within its reach. At times, it is a pugnacious species and once a pair has established their right to a stretch of water, they are very intolerant of the presence of others of their kind. Its food consists of tiny fishes and various aquatic insects, larvae and other organisms.

© Neeraj Mishra

± 15 CM, FRESH WATER IN OPEN COUNTRY, SLOW-MOVING STREAMS AND CANALS

LCR | LC

## Pied Kingfisher

*Ceryle rudis* कौरिल्ली किलकिला

A distinctive, medium-sized kingfisher with black-and-white plumage and a speckled body, the Pied kingfisher is a common bird in the plains. It inhabits all kinds of waterbodies with patches of open water without floating vegetation, but avoids small streams and other smaller waterbodies in the mountains, confining itself to river banks. It has a voracious appetite. Pied kingfisher has a strong flight and is often seen flying over water at about 10 feet to 20 feet above the surface. On sighting a shoal of fish below, it checks itself mid-air, and hovers with the wings vibrating rapidly and the bill pointing perpendicularly downwards, as if taking aim. The Pied kingfisher is a common bird of Lucknow.

± 25 CM, STILL FRESHWATER PONDS, SLOW-MOVING RIVERS AND STREAMS

CR | LC

# MEROPIDAE (Bee-eaters)

- Green Bee-eater
- Blue-tailed Bee-eater

Bee-eaters are brightly coloured birds, easily identifiable by their large head and short legs. They primarily feed on insects, mostly large flying insects, by making short, swift sallies like a flycatcher, from an exposed perch, such as a telegraph wire, branch, post or a treetop. Most bee-eaters are gregarious and nest in burrows tunnelled into vertical sandy banks, often at the side of a river or in flat ground. As they mostly live in colonies, a large number of nest holes may be seen together.

# Green Bee-eater

± 17 CM, OPEN COUNTRY WITH SCATTERED TREES, GRAZING LAND

CR | LC

*Merops orientalis* हरा पतरंगा

One of the most common birds of India, the Green Bee-eater is known for its beautiful plumage and form. It is a small, slenderly-built bird of bright green colour with a rather long, curved black beak. The bird spends its life hawking insects from a perch, telegraph wires being its favourite, to which it returns after every flight, usually carrying a captured insect, which is battered to death before being eaten. It also settles on trees, low bushes and walls, but it only visits the ground for nesting purposes. Its small and weak feet render the bird incapable of movement by walking or hopping. It is fairly common in Lucknow.

# Blue-tailed Bee-eater

*Merops philippinus* नील दुम पतरंगा

± 25 CM, OPEN COUNTRY AND CULTIVATION NEAR WATER

LCR | LC

This bee-eater is mostly found in well-cultivated areas and open country, provided it is not too dry. The Blue-tailed bee-eater has a distinctive appearance because of its blue rump and tail, and a chestnut throat. Like the other bee-eaters in the family, it perches on open elevated resting places, such as tall, half-withered trees standing in water or on telegraph wires, and continually darts into the air to capture its prey. Its food primarily consists of insects, chiefly dragon-flies and bees. Known for its elegant flight, this bird is usually seen in small flocks. Its call is similar to liquid rattles and trills. It is commonly found in Lucknow during summer months.

# CUCULIDAE (Cuckoos, Malkohas and Coucals)

Cuckoos are medium-sized slender birds with fairly long necks and decurved bills. Almost all cuckoos are arboreal and prefer foliage. Known for their tuneful calls, males of most cuckoos are very noisy in the breeding season, calling frequently during the day and often in night. Generally, for most of their lives, cuckoos live as solitary birds and are seldom found in pairs or groups. Cuckoos are known as brood parasite, a unique feature. They are usually found in well-wooded areas and large gardens.

Malkohas are larger than cuckoos with plumper bodies. Coucals are large, skulking birds. Mostly terrestrial, they can be spotted frequenting dense undergrowth.

- Pied Cuckoo or Jacobin Cuckoo
- Common Hawk-cuckoo
- Indian Cuckoo
- Common Cuckoo
- Chestnut-winged Cuckoo
- Grey-bellied Cuckoo
- Sirkeer Malkoha
- Asian Koel
- Greater Coucal
- Lesser Coucal

# Jacobin or Pied Cuckoo

± 32 CM, WELL-WOODED AREAS NEAR WETLANDS, URBAN GARDENS AND PARKS

LCS | LC

*Clamator jacobinus* अबलक चातक

A black-and-white bird, the Jacobin cuckoo is known to visit gardens and light forests. It is popularly known as the Rainbird as it migrates over large areas across northern India around summer when monsoon approaches. It is one of the few migratory birds that come to the Indian subcontinent from Africa to breed. It is believed that the bird uses monsoon winds to assist its flight during this migration. As per a historical account, it is fairly abundant in Lucknow, but William Jesse claims that it does not appear till the beginning of June, after the rains have commenced, and that he has never seen it after September, except for a single bird in November 1901.[1,2]

[1] Reid, George. *Stray Feathers*. 1897, p. 556.
[2] Ibid. 1903, p. 58.

# Common Hawk-cuckoo

± 33 CM, URBAN GARDENS, PARKS AND WELL-WOODED COUNTRY

**LCR** LC

*Hierococcyx varius* सामान्य पपीहा

The Common Hawk-cuckoo is a bird of the well-wooded country and it is almost entirely arboreal and rarely descends to the ground. The bird is known for its remarkable voice. Like most of the cuckoos during the breeding season, the male hawk-cuckoo becomes extremely vocal and produces a repetitive three-note call. This call is exceedingly loud and shrill and can be heard across a considerable distance. It is also known as the brain-fever bird on account of this loud cry. The Common Hawk-cuckoos feed mainly on insects, and is a specialised feeder that can handle hairy caterpillars. These birds are fairly common in Lucknow and can be easily spotted in gardens and well-wooded areas.

# Sirkeer Malkoha

± 42 CM, OPEN FORESTS, SCRUBLANDS, DENSE GROWTH AROUND HABITATION

LCR LC

*Taccocua leschenaultia* लालमुखी मालकोहा

The Sirkeer is, by preference, a bird of scrub-jungles, secondary growth and large gardens. The adult male is mostly sandy brown and has a cherry-red bill. It is a terrestrial bird, usually found walking about on the ground amongst bushes or thick cover, in search of a very mixed diet of fruits, seeds, berries, grasshoppers, beetles and other small insects. The bird is known for its liking for lizards. It is a poor flier, preferring to thread its way into the centre of a thicket. Sirkeer is a silent bird and prefers to live and move through the undergrowth. It is not so common in Lucknow.

© Rajesh Panwar

# Asian Koel

± 45 CM, URBAN GARDENS, OPEN WOODLANDS AND CULTIVATION

**CR** LC

## *Eudynamys scolopaceus* कोयल

The most familiar and common cuckoo, the Asian koel is a bird better known by its sweet call. The male bird has a glossy bluish-black appearance while the female, in contrast, has brownish and rufous streaks. It is a bird of groves and gardens, haunting patches of large trees in whose shady boughs it finds shelter and food. It never descends to the ground. A known brood parasite, it lays its eggs in the nests of crows and other hosts, who unknowingly raise its young. Its usual diet consists of fruit, especially of banyan, peepul and other figs, and often snails too. The song of the male is a repeated 'koo-Ooo koo-Ooo koo-Ooo' while the female makes a shrill 'kik-kik-kik' call. The bird is widely referred in Indian poetry.

Asian Koel (Male)

Asian Koel (Female)

# Greater Coucal

*Centropus sinensis* बड़ा महोक

The Greater coucal is also known as the Crow pheasant owing to its appearance—a cross between a crow and pheasant. It is a common ground feeder in the plains in the city areas. It avoids forests and is found in cultivated areas, bush jungles or wastelands. It can be seen along village roadsides or banks of rivers and canals. It walks slowly like a pheasant and hunts on the ground. Wasps, beetles, caterpillars, grasshoppers, small lizards, snakes and other similar food includes its diet. Mostly terrestrial, it also perches on top of bushes, above the low-growing vegetation.

± 48 CM, AREAS WITH MIXED VEGETATION AND DENSE UNDERGROWTH AROUND WETLANDS

CR | LC

# PSITTACIDAE (Parakeets)

Parrots or parakeets are amongst the most familiar birds in our lives. They are mostly forest birds but are found in practically any type of habitat with numerous large trees. They have been observed to live alone as well as in pairs, small groups or families. They are strong fliers, largely arboreal and gregarious, and prefer open grasslands and well-wooded tracts. Nearly all parrots make simple nests in tree holes. They are popular pets due to their colourful patterns and cute mannerisms, including picking things up with their feet and climbing with their bills. Several species of the parrot family enjoy popularity because of their ability to mimic human speech.

- Rose-ringed Parakeet
- Plum-headed Parakeet
- Alexandrine Parakeet

# Rose-ringed Parakeet

## *Psittacula krameri* सामान्य तोता

The Rose-ringed parakeet is one of the most well-known species in India. This abundant species can be seen in pairs during the breeding season and forms parties and flocks at other times. Generally, this parakeet is arboreal and a wonderful climber, equally at home in every position, but flies down to feed on crops and garden plants, and occasionally settles on the ground to pick up food. The Rose-ringed parakeet has the habit of an evening roosting flight; flock after flock hurrying in succession along the same line to some patch of trees where they roost in company with flocks of crows and mynahs.

In Lucknow, heritage properties, such as The Residency, National Botanical Research Institute, Raj Bhavan, with their old, mature trees, hold a sizeable number of this parakeet species.

± 42 CM, WELL-WOODED AREAS, ORCHARDS AND CULTIVATION

CR | LC

# Plum-headed Parakeet

## *Psittacula cyanocephala* टुइयाँ तोता

The Plum-headed parakeet is a beautiful bird and to a large extent, a forest bird, though it is also found in well-wooded areas and cultivated lands. Like the other parakeets, it is a social bird, found in parties. It feeds on seeds and fruits of forest trees, but very seldom descends to the ground. Its strong, darting flight pattern is faster than that of the other two species described in this work. Once common, now they are found only in a few isolated, well-wooded patches on the outskirts of Lucknow.

± 36 CM, FORESTS AND WELL-WOODED AREAS

LCR | LC

# Alexandrine Parakeet

± 52 CM, DECIDUOUS FORESTS AND WELL-WOODED AREAS

LCR LC

*Psittacula eupatria* हीरामन तोता

The largest of all the parakeet species in the city, the Alexandrine parakeet has a deep-red shoulder patch, making it easy to spot the bird. It is found in any type of habitat that have numerous large trees. It lives in flocks, which often collect to roost in large avenues and groves of trees. The members of the flock are known to gather in the evenings, flying off to roosting places, travelling many miles to find a spot at a great height. While flying, it frequently utters a loud shrill call.

# APODIDAE (Swifts)

Swifts are birds with a drab plumage and scythe- or sickle-shaped wings. An aerial species, they spend most of their lives on the wing. The shape of their wings makes high-speed flight easy for them. As the name Apodidae (without feet) suggests, they have tiny feet and, as a consequence, are unable to perch. Mostly found near water, they are known for being peculiar nest-makers. They often use their saliva as glue to hold their nests together.

- Asian Palm Swift
- House or Little Swift

# Asian Palm Swift

± 12 CM, LIGHT FORESTS WITH PALM TREES AND CULTIVATION

CR | LC

*Cypsiurus balasiensis* तड़ी अबाबील बतासी

The Asian Palm swift is a small, slender swift with long, narrow, sickle-shaped wings and very long, deeply-forked tail, which, when folded, looks thin and pointed. This quaint little swift is mainly found where palm trees are grown as it roosts in the fronds of the palm trees. It is a highly gregarious bird, and can sometimes be seen in mixed parties. The bird spends its life hawking for insects, including small beetles in its vicinity, flying around in a rather irregular flight, slower than most other species of swifts. The Asian Palm swift is a local bird of Lucknow and often nests in thatched roofs as well.

© Kallol Mukherjee

# TYTONIDAE, STRIGIDAE (Owls)

Owls are birds of various sizes with a fairly large and round head. The external physical characteristics are short, parrot-like beak, large eyes and uncommonly well-developed ears. They are nocturnal birds which fly with barely any sound owing to a special feather structure, and have particularly acute hearing. Owls make their nests in tree holes. They greatly vary in size across the species of this family. The Barn owl is very different in size and shape from the Spotted owlet, which is smaller in size and has a different shape. Almost all species of owls are effective pest controllers.

- Spotted Owlet
- Jungle Owlet
- Brown Fish Owl
- Oriental Scops Owl
- Mottled Wood Owl
- Indian/Rock/Bengal Eagle-owl
- Barn Owl
- Brown Boobook or Brown Hawk-owl
- Indian Scops Owl

# Spotted Owlet

## *Athene brama* सामान्य खूसट

A small and stocky bird, the Spotted owlet prefers gardens and well-wooded areas. This crepuscular and nocturnal bird usually lives in pairs or small parties. After spending the day in a tree cavity, ruins or on leafy branches, it emerges around dusk, often with a diagnostic, harsh and chattering call. It often perches close to the glare of lamps and streetlights to feast on the insects that gather around them. It also hunts around gardens. Once widespread across most urban areas, its numbers have come down significantly, mainly due to unsustainable development activities. The loss of old, mature trees and abandoned architecture are two of the prime reasons for the decline in their population in Lucknow.

± 21 CM, AROUND HUMAN HABITATION, CULTIVATION

CR LC

# Jungle Owlet

## *Glaucidium radiatum* जंगली डूनडूल

Also known as the Barred Jungle owlet, the Jungle owlet is a small owl. It has a noticeable, round head and fine bars all over the body. The Jungle owl prefers to spend most of the day in some high leafy branch or a tree cavity. It is one of the most audible owls during the daytime. It is found either alone, in pairs or small groups, and is usually identified by its calls at dawn and dusk. Several types of insects, small rodents, lizards and frogs form a part of their diet. It is commonly found in Lucknow.

± 20 CM, OPEN FORESTS AND HUMAN HABITATION

CR LC

# Brown Fish Owl

± 55 CM, WELL-WOODED AREAS NEAR WATER

LCR | LC

*Ketupa zeylonensis* अमराई का उल्लू

This large owl is always found in the vicinity of water and its food, which includes birds and small mammals, mostly fish and crabs, which it catches at the edge of rivers and streams. The Brown Fish owl sleeps by day in some large, heavily-foliaged tree or on rocky cliff, and with the fall of dusk, wings its way to the neighbouring waterbody, uttering a strange screaming call. It keeps an eye out for its prey from a perch overlooking the water, such as a stump or rock on the edge or in the middle of a stream, and scoops up fishes just below the surface of the water. It often flies up and down, sometimes almost skimming the water.

# Mottled Wood Owl

*Strix ocellata* चित्तरा बन उल्लू

± 48 CM, OPEN WOODED AREAS AND GROVES AROUND VILLAGES

**LCR** LC

The Mottled Wood owl is a fairly common bird of lightly-wooded gardens. It is a large owl with a typical 'owl face' but no ear tufts. Most beautifully barred and mottled in brownish-black and white, this bird is found in the well-wooded country where large ancient trees provide it with holes to nest in, and cover to spend the day. It sleeps through the day in shady refuge, emerging at nightfall to hunt the surrounding area. It lives entirely on squirrels, rats and mice, and is one of the most beneficial birds to Indian agriculture.

In Lucknow, areas within cantonment and some of the heritage venues with plenty of large trees are the best sites to sight the bird.

© Dr Vivek Banerjee

# Indian/Rock/Bengal Eagle-owl

*Bubo bengalensis* सामान्य घुग्घू

± 62 CM, OPEN WOODED AREAS AROUND VILLAGES, CLIFFS AND SEMI-DESERTS

**LCR** LC

It is a widespread, large-sized, dark-brown owl with tufts on its head. Mainly nocturnal, it inhabits well-wooded but open and cultivated country. The bird mostly feeds on rodents but also hunts smaller birds, including partridges and doves. Field rats and mice form a considerable proportion of the owl's diet in agricultural areas. This large owl, with a distinctive face, large forward-facing eyes, horns and a deep resonant call, is associated with a number of superstitions. Locally found in this region, the Indian Eagle-owl is also considered a bird of ill omen just like the other large owls.

© Rajesh Panwar

# Brown Hawk-owl

± 32 CM, WELL-WOODED AREAS AND FORESTS

LCR | LC

*Ninox scutulata* भूरा बाज़ उल्लू

Also known as the Brown Boobook or the Hume's Hawk-owl, the Brown Hawk-owl is a dark brown, medium-sized, hawk-like owl with a round head and no ear tufts. It feeds mainly on large insects, such as beetles and grasshoppers, frogs, lizards, small birds and mice. Occasionally, it also feeds on small bats and crabs. The Brown Hawk-owl hunts at dusk, using a perch on a tree stump or post to look for prey. It has also been observed jumping up to catch passing insects in its claws, and hawking insects in the air like nightjars. This bird is not found commonly in the city.

# Barn Owl

*Tyto alba* करेल उल्लू

± 36 CM, OPEN COUNTRY, AROUND VILLAGES, OLD OR ABANDONED BUILDINGS

CR | LC

The Barn owl is a medium-sized, pale bird with long wings and a short, squarish tail. The pale face, with its heart shape and black eyes, give the flying bird a distinctive appearance. It is the most widespread land bird species in the world, found in every continent, except Antarctica. Like most owls, the Barn owl is nocturnal, relying on its acute sense of hearing when hunting in complete darkness. It prefers open country habitats, such as farmlands or grasslands, where it feeds on small mammals. It is also found in the cities, nesting on secluded ledges of tall buildings.

# CAPRIMULGIDAE (Nightjars)

Nightjars are also known as Goatsuckers as it was once thought that they used their wide mouths to milk goats. A ridiculous superstition, which has no foundation in fact. The word for goat-milker in Latin is *caprimulgus*. Nightjars are nocturnal birds with cryptically-coloured plumage. It is quite difficult to spot the bird even during the day as it roosts among the leaf litter on the ground. The most striking feature of the nightjar is the large size of the mouth accompanied by a remarkably small beak, which is fringed on either side by long, stiff bristles. There are several nightjars in India, which are difficult to identify without a close study of indicators, such as call notes and the arrangement of spots on the wings and tail.

- Large-tailed Nightjar
- Indian Nightjar

# Large-tailed Nightjar

## *Caprimulgus macrurus* बड़ पूँछ छपका

This bird has a number of other names: the Long-tailed nightjar, the White-tailed nightjar and the Coffin-bird. It has slender wings, short legs and a very small bill. The Large-tail nightjar feeds on flying insects it catches on the wing, either at night or at dawn/dusk. The smallness of its feet is attributed to the fact that it procures all its food while on the wing, and when not flying, it remains motionless, squatting either on the ground or on the bough of a tall tree. This Lucknow bird usually nests on the ground.

± 32 CM, WELL-WOODED AREAS AND FOREST EDGES

LCR | LC

# Indian Nightjar

## *Caprimulgus asiaticus* सामान्य छपका

Also known as the Common Indian nightjar or the Little Indian nightjar, it is a large, softly-plumaged, dull-mottled, brown-and-grey bird. It is a bird of the plains, and open and cultivated country, where it is found in gardens and groves. It spends the day on the ground sleeping in secluded spot under a bush or a tree, and becomes active at dusk, being entirely nocturnal in its habits. Is mostly feeds on insects, moths and beetles. The Indian nightjar is not commonly spotted in Lucknow.

© Amit Mishra

± 24 CM, OPEN SCRUBLANDS, CULTIVATION AND LIGHT FORESTS

NCR | LC

# COLUMBIDAE

## (Pigeons and Doves)

There is not much difference in the general appearance of pigeons and doves except the size; pigeons are slightly larger than doves. They are among the most familiar birds found around human habitation. For the most part, they are arboreal in their habits, and hence, probably, the peculiarly short legs. Certain species, however, have taken to living on the ground, and these species have much longer legs. The green pigeon is strictly arboreal. Some species are highly gregarious outside the breeding season, especially during harvest time. They are stout-bodied birds with short necks and short slender bills, that in some species feature fleshy ceres. They are excellent fliers, mainly due to the lift provided by their large wings.

- Common Pigeon or Rock Dove
- Spotted Dove
- Laughing Dove
- Eurasian Collared-dove
- Red Collared-dove
- Oriental Turtle Dove
- Yellow-footed Green Pigeon
- Orange-breasted Green Pigeon
- Emerald Dove

# Rock Pigeon

*Columba livia* सामान्य कबूतर

The Rock dove, also known as the Blue rock pigeon, ranks with the house crow and sparrow as one of the most familiar birds of the urban landscape. It keeps to human habitations, and almost every town has its resident pigeon population. The Rock pigeon crowds streets and public squares, living on discarded food and offerings of birdseed. It nests on buildings and window ledges. In the countryside, it makes its nest in barns and grain towers, under bridges, and on natural cliffs. Warehouse sheds, office and factory buildings, and railway stations are few of the other favoured spots. Here, collectively, they occupy rafters and cornices, and become an unmitigated nuisance on account of the mess they make.

± 33 CM, TOWNS, VILLAGES AND AROUND HUMAN HABITATION

CR | LC

# Oriental Turtle Dove

*Streptopelia orientalis* काल्हक फाख्ता

Also known as Rufous Turtle dove, this bird is a common resident of open forests and cultivated lands in the foothills. Its habitat varies, though it breeds in well-wooded but open habitats. Its back is characterized by a remarkable brown scale pattern. It is often seen in pairs. The male dove sings in a low tone, 'de de popoo'. The song is also used to call females and declare territory. When a male chases a female or indicates its nest, it cries 'kur kur'. It is a winter visitor in Lucknow.

± 33 CM, OPEN FORESTS, ESPECIALLY NEAR CULTIVATION

CR | LC

# Spotted Dove

## *Streptopelia chinensis* चित्रोख फाख्ता

A common bird of the well-wooded and cultivated open country, the Spotted dove is found in gardens as well as in urban areas. It moves around in pairs or small groups, foraging on the ground for grass seeds, grains and fallen fruits. It may, however, catch insects occasionally, and has been recorded feeding on winged termites. They take off from the ground collectively with an explosive flutter, and sometimes, glide down to a perch. A common bird in this region, the Spotted dove coos loudly and quite often. The call goes like 'coo-a-roooo'.

# Laughing Dove

## *Streptopelia senegalensis* टूटरूं

The Laughing dove, also known as the Senegal dove or the Little Brown dove, is a small, long-tailed dove. It is found in scrub forests, dry farmlands as well as in areas of human habitation, and is a common bird in the city. Usually seen in pairs or small parties and rarely in larger groups, it forages near shrubs, and feeds on fruits and seeds from plants. The Laughing dove's song resembles a human laugh and can be heard all-year round. Though during the day, the calls are less frequent.

± 30 CM, CULTIVATION, HABITATION AND OPEN FORESTS

CR LC

± 27 CM, DRY CULTIVATION AND SCRUB-COVERED AREAS

LCR LC

# Eurasian Collared-dove

*Streptopelia decaocto* धवर फाख्ता

Also known as the Indian Ring dove, it is a pretty large dove, which loves cultivated but dry open country, abounding in groves of trees providing shelter from the heat of the day. Thorny scrub, babul and dhak jungles are its favourite roosting places. It is found abundantly in the neighbourhood of human habitations. When not breeding, it usually forages in flocks on the ground, and sometimes, looks for berries among tree branches and shrubs. One of the commonest doves of the plains, the Eurasian Collared-dove is plentiful in Lucknow.

± 32 CM, DRY OPEN COUNTRY, CULTIVATION AND GROVES

# Red Collared-dove

*Streptopelia tranquebarica* इंट कोहरी फाख्ता

The Red Collared-dove or the Red Turtle dove is a small dove and one of the least abundant of the doves in Lucknow. It is a dweller of the cultivated open country and is seldom found in the immediate proximity of human habitations. It prefers wooded tracts of land, such as canal or roadside tree plantations, and avoids desert regions. It usually lives either single or in pairs, and sometimes, in large flocks, in association with other doves. The Red Collared-dove gleans grain, seeds and vegetable matter on the ground. It often perches and suns on leafless branches and overhead wires.

© Neeraj Mishra

± 23 CM, LIGHTLY-WOODED AREAS AND OPEN COUNTRY

LCR | LC

# Yellow-footed Green Pigeon

± 33 CM, HUMAN HABITATIONS, CLIFFS AND RUINS

LCR LC

*Treron phoenicopterus* सामान्य हरियल

Also known as Yellow-legged Green pigeon, it is a stout, yellowish, olive-green and ashy-grey pigeon with a lilac patch on the shoulders. This pigeon is exclusively arboreal and seldom, if ever, descends to the ground. Found in well-wooded open country as well as forests, the bird is also frequently found in the vicinity of towns and villages, and even gardens. It deftly climbs on to the twigs of fruit-bearing trees, often clinging upside down to get at some fig or berry. The birds spend the day doing rounds of fruit trees, resting at intervals on the topmost branches of a dry or leafless one. Their food consists entirely of fruits and berries, predominantly wild figs, but it also feeds on buds and shoots. The Yellow-footed Green pigeon is one of the commonest of Green pigeons found in Lucknow.

# Emerald Dove

## *Chalcophaps indica* पन्ना फाख्ता

± 27 CM, BROADLEAVED FOREST AND WELL-WOODED AREAS

NCS | LC

This charming little dove is essentially a forest bird, found throughout the greater part of India, where there is sufficient rainfall. Though normally it moves about in a rather sedate and graceful manner, it is capable of great speed when disturbed or roused by white ants. Naturally, like all its family, the bird is entirely vegetarian with one exception, it captures and eats termites greedily. The Emerald dove is a common summer visitor.

# GRUIDAE (Cranes)

Cranes are large, tall and long-shanked birds. They are known to fly with their neck and feet stretched straight and in a 'V' formation, like geese. Cranes inhabit a wide variety of open habitats, but most species prefer wet areas.

There are 15 species of cranes in the world found in all continents, except the Arctic. Out of the three species of cranes found in Lucknow, two are migratory. Demoiselle cranes undertake one of the toughest migrations in the world. They gather in flocks of up to 400 birds and prepare for their flight to their winter range. During their arduous journey, they cross the Himalayan Mountains to get to their overwintering grounds in India. Many die from fatigue, hunger and predation by Golden eagles.

This family of birds has a generalised diet, everything from leaves, nuts, berries, insects to small vertebrates is part of their diet. Besides, they have a preference for rhizomes, tubers, aquatic invertebrate and very small fish and fingerlings. They hardly eat big fish. They typically nest on the ground with a fairly large nest, a simple mound of vegetation topped by a shallow depression. They prefer islands, shallow lakes or waterlogged paddy fields to protect themselves from predators. Their ability to sing sonorous and trumpet-like notes is usually attributed to the peculiar formation of its trachea, which after exiting the lower end of the neck passes backwards, and is received in a hollow space formed by the bony walls of the breast bone. Cranes are strictly monogamous and their elaborate courtship display reinforces existing pair bonds. Once mated, the pair remains together for life. However, pairs unsuccessful in breeding attempts will often separate and the birds find new mates. Cranes are said to be elegant ambassadors of the open field. Their haunting cries and courtship dance display has significant status in many cultures from time immemorial. By eliminating undesirable weed and harmful insect stock, cranes play an important role in controlling pests, hence, are aptly called 'farmer's friend'.

- Common Crane
- Sarus Crane
- Demoiselle Crane

# Sarus Crane

*Antigone antigone* सारस

± 155 CM, CULTIVATION AND WELL-WATERED COUNTRY AND MARSHES

LCR Vulnerable

The state bird of Uttar Pradesh, the Sarus crane is one of the tallest flying birds in the world. It is also known as an iconic bird of freshwater wetlands. There are 15 known species of cranes worldwide. Out of which, 6 species occur in India. The Sarus is an elegant steel-grey bird with a height up to 6 feet.

It prefers a combination of flooded, partially-flooded and dry ground for foraging, roosting and nesting. It is omnivorous, feeding on a variety of roots and tubers as well as invertebrates and amphibians. In some locations, the bird disperses seasonally in response to available water. Breeding pairs maintain discrete territories in areas with adequate water supply throughout the year, while non-breeding birds are generally found in flocks that prefer larger wetlands to roost. The bird is being increasingly forced to use suboptimal rice paddies as breeding habitat because of the deterioration and destruction of its natural wetland habitat. The bird, despite rampant and unsustainable development, is active in many states and is also trying to hold on to its habitat within Lucknow. The few natural wetlands in the outskirts of Lucknow seem to be the last home for the bird here.

The Sarus crane is also an important indicator species, indicating, at a given point of time, the health of the wetlands on which its very existence depends. They can be spotted in the last remaining areas of its habitat on the outer limits of the city—though not many—in farmlands in the vicinity of the Indira Gandhi Canal and the waterbodies around the Sanjay Gandhi Post Graduate Institute on the Raiberali road.

# Common Crane

*Grus grus* सामान्य क्रौंच

A big, slate-grey bird with long neck and legs, the Common crane arrives in our country during autumn and leaves after winter. Black markings on the head and neck and the black legs distinguish it from the Sarus crane. Found in parties or flocks, which usually pass the middle of the day and the whole night in open riverbeds or lakes, the Common crane stays vigilant against any unwanted surprises. It flies back to cultivated lands to feed in the morning and evening. The Common crane may either forage on land or in shallow water, probing around with its bills for any edible organism. Although crops may be damaged by the species, it mostly consumes waste grain in winter from previously harvested fields, and so actually benefits farmers by cleaning fields for reuse in the following season. The Common crane is omnivorous, as are all cranes. It largely eats plant matter, including roots, rhizomes, tubers, stems, leaves, fruits and seeds. It stays on the ground only. Occasional sightings have been recorded in Lucknow.

© Dr Vivek Banerjee

± 115 CM, CULTIVATION, MARSHES, LARGE RIVERS AND RESERVOIRS

NCW | LC

# Demoiselle Crane

*Grus virgo* कुर्जा

The Demoiselle crane is slightly smaller than the Common crane but has similar plumage. It is a grey bird and is easily distinguishable from the other cranes because of the white plume of soft feathers behind each eye and the black under the surface of the neck, ending in black plumes forming pendant over the breast. This crane is a common winter visitor to northern India. During migration, large flocks make stopovers in cultivated areas, as in the wintering grounds. It has been observed that the migratory flocks can have up to 400 birds in the beginning, but swells to thousands when they arrive at the wintering destinations.

It is known for its loud trumpeting call, higher-pitched than the Common crane. Like other cranes, it has a dancing display, though more balletic with less leaping.

© Rajesh Panwar

± 95 CM, CULTIVATION AND LARGE RIVERS WITH SANDBANKS

NCW | LC

# RALLIDAE
## (Rails, Crakes and Coots)

This is a group of small- to medium-sized birds with moderate to long legs meant for wading. The Common coot is the only bird in this group which has some characteristics similar to that of ducks, and inhabits waterbodies. Most of the birds in the family, barring a few, are terrestrial and can be found in marshes. Since they are not good fliers, they fly only short distances. They are more often heard than seen, especially during the early hours of the day.

- Brown Crake
- White-breasted Waterhen
- Purple Swamphen
- Common Moorhen
- Baillon's Crake
- Watercock
- Common or Eurasian Coot

# Brown Crake

± 28 CM, WETLANDS EDGES WITH COVER AND UNDERGROWTH

LCR LC

## *Amaurornis akool* भूरी क्रेक

Also known as the Brown Bush-hen, this bird is dusky-brown in colour. Its genus name *Amaurornis* comes from the Greek words *amauros*, which means dusky or brown and *ornis* which means bird. It is a round, softly-coloured inhabitant of wetlands, rice fields, wet shrubby areas and reedbeds. Despite its preference for sheltered habitats, the Brown crake is one of the bolder rails and can be seen wandering in the open. It feeds primarily on invertebrates, insects, worms and seeds, grass and berries. As it forages, it constantly cocks its tail upwards and downwards.

© Rajesh Panwar

# White-breasted Waterhen

*Amaurornis phoenicurus* सफ़ेद छाती जलमुर्गी

± 32 CM, WETLANDS EDGES WITH COVER AND UNDERGROWTH

CR | LC

The White-breasted waterhen is a slaty, dark bird with a clean white face, breast and belly. It is somewhat bolder than most other rails and is often seen stepping slowly with its tail cocked upright. Usually seen alone or in pairs, they forage slowly along the edge of a waterbody, mainly on the ground, but sometimes, clambering up on low vegetation, in open marshes and even drains near busy roads. It is a common species in this region.

# Purple Swamphen

## *Porphyrio porphyrio* जामुनी जलमुर्गी

A large gleaming bluish-purple bird, the Purple swamphen has a red bill, and red legs and feet with long toes. The tail is flicked up often, revealing fluffy white 'underpants'. This purple coot is found wherever there are large swamps and lakes with plenty of rushes, bushes and weeds. It lives in small parties which spend their lives chiefly within the reed beds, threading their way through the labyrinth of vegetation with remarkable ease, and clinging to the reeds and twigs with its huge feet. This resident of the region mainly feeds on plant and vegetable matter.

± 48 CM, WETLANDS WITH EXTENSIVE REED BEDS

**LCR** LC

# Common Moorhen

## *Gallinula chloropus* सामान्य जलमुर्गी

Also known as the Eurasian or Indian moorhen, it lives in well-vegetated marshes, ponds, canals and other wetlands. The species is not found in the polar regions or the tropical rainforests. The Common moorhen consumes a wide variety of vegetable material and small aquatic creatures. foraging beside or in the water, sometimes walking on lilypads or upending in the water to feed. It is usually secretive, though can become tame in some areas. In Lucknow, this is a commonly breeding bird, usually seen in marshlands, well-vegetated lakes, and even in city parks.

© Neeraj Mishra

± 35 CM, MARSHES AND REED-EDGED POOLS

**LCR** LC

# Watercock

*Gallicrex cinerea* कोरा

± 43 CM (M) & 36 CM (F), MARSHES AND FLOODED FIELDS

LCS | LC

Known as 'Kora', the watercock is a waterbird in the rail and crake family, and is found in the more swampy areas. The body of this rail is flattened laterally to allow easier passage through reeds or undergrowth. It has long toes and a short tail. Just like Baillon's crake, the watercock probes with its bill in mud or shallow water and picks up food by sight. It mainly feeds on insects, small fish, and seeds, and forages on the ground. Though it is quite a secretive bird, it is sometimes seen out in the open. Generally a noisy bird, especially at dawn and dusk, it has a loud, gulping call.

© Amit Mishra

# Common or Eurasian Coot

± 38 CM, MARSHES AND REED-EDGED POOLS

LCR | LC

*Fulica atra* टिकरी

The Common or Eurasian coot is a widespread waterbird, which has a completely black body, with a white mark on the top of its head. It is found in flocks and frequents open waters, such as lakes, tanks and slowly-moving rivers. It is mainly a migrant species, but is also a resident species in some parts of the country. The Common coot has large yellow feet with spread toes to help them grip branches and walk on mud without sinking. It prefers open water and not reed beds, except when breeding.

This omnivorous bird finds its food by the edge of the waterbody it haunts. Its food consists largely of vegetable matter, which is accquired both on the surface and by diving, but it also eats small fish, insects and molluscs. It is known to be quite aggressive to other birds, at times.

# PTEROCLIDAE (Sandgrouse)

Sandgrouse have small, pigeon-like heads and necks with sturdy compact bodies. They are essentially ground-dwelling birds restricted to treeless, open country, such as plains, savannahs and semi-deserts. Though principally seed-eaters, they also consume green shoots and leaves, bulbs and berries, and insects, like ants and termites, during the breeding period. They are gregarious and form flocks of up to 100 birds. As a consequence of their dry diet, they need to visit water sources regularly. Two species of sandgrouse have been spotted in the city from time to time.

© Rajesh Panwar

- Chestnut-bellied Sandgrouse
- Painted Sandgrouse

# Chestnut-bellied Sandgrouse

± 38 CM, MARSHES AND REED-EDGED POOLS

**LCR** LC

*Pterocles exustus* कुहार भटतीतर

Also known as the Indian or the Common Indian sandgrouse, this is a large, plump, dove-like bird with a pointed tail, found in sparse, bushy and arid land. Though it lives in hot and arid climates, it is highly reliant on water. A vegetarian bird, it prefers leguminous weed seeds and seldom eats grass seeds. This bird is strong on the wing and seems to prefer to remain in open country. It does not rely on escape cover as its natural protective coloration blends in well with earth and rocks.

© Rajesh Panwar

# SCOLOPACIDAE (Sandpipers, Godwits, Stints, Snipes, Curlews)

Birds in this category are commonly referred as waders. They are often confusing to the eye because of similarity in shape, however, they differ in size. Among the larger waders, the largest of them all is the Eurasian curlew (*Numenius arquata*), which is about the size of the mallard (*Anas platyrhynchos*), while stints and sanderlings represent the smaller category of waders. They are fast-flying birds, generally found on marshy grounds.

With long legs and an extraordinarily long bill, godwits are the easiest waders to identify. They relish snails, slugs, frog spawn, insects and other creatures living in the mud and slime.

Snipes relish worms, insect larvae and other squishy things they find in the mud with their long, probing bills.

Dunlin and knots are small- to medium-sized, rather plump waders, with smaller bills and legs.

- Black-tailed Godwit
- Whimbrel
- Common Redshank
- Common Greenshank
- Spotted Redshank
- Marsh Sandpiper
- Wood Sandpiper
- Green Sandpiper
- Common Sandpiper
- Ruff
- Little Stint
- Temminck's Stint
- Dunlin
- Common Snipe
- Pin-tailed Snipe

# Black-tailed Godwit

± 44 CM, MUD BANKS OF FRESHWATER PONDS AND LAKES

LCR LC

*Limosa limosa* बड़ा गुदेरा

The Black-tailed Godwit is a medium-sized wader, which has a very long bill, with a pink base. This bird is fairly common and breeds in grassy wetlands. It is fairly common and can be found in fresh and brackish marshes, and on adjacent tidal flats. Highly gregarious, it feeds mainly by wading in deep water, probing with its long bill. It is a purely migratory bird, arriving by October and departing by April. Some birds linger on for a longer period. The shallow wetlands in the outskirts of Lucknow are the best sites to watch the bird during the winter months.

# Common Redshank

*Tringa totanus* छोटा सूरमा चौबाहा

This stocky, brown wader with bright red legs inhabits freshwater and coastal wetlands. The Common redshank is a wary bird and often alerts the other birds with its loud, fluty, whistled calls. It bobs its tail when nervous and then flies to exposing the secondary feathers on its wings and the rump patch, both of which are white. Like most waders, it feeds in muddy shallows, probing and picking with its bill for small insects, spiders, worms, molluscs and crustaceans, besides small fish and tadpoles. Its feeding habits depend on the season. The Common redshank is a winter visitor.

© Amit Mishra

± 28 CM, BANKS OF RIVERS AND LAKES AND MARSHES

LCW LC

# Spotted Redshank

*Tringa erythropus* बड़ा सूरमा चौबाहा

The Spotted redshank is slimmer, has longer legs and is more elegant than the other species of redshanks. It breeds in arctic bogs and swamps. Varied wetland habitats serve as migration destinations for the bird. Usually seen alone or in small groups, it is sometimes seen as part of large flocks, especially on wintering grounds. It often forages in deeper waters than the other redshanks, by swimming and upending. Its food consists of aquatic insects and their larvae, terrestrial flying insects, small crustaceans, molluscs, worms, fish and amphibians.

± 32 CM, BANKS OF SHALLOW RIVERS AND LAKES

NCW LC

## Marsh Sandpiper

### *Tringa stagnatilis* छोटा टिमटिमा चौबाहा

The Marsh sandpiper is a slender, pale, tail-bobbing wading bird with a fine, needle-like bill. It frequents inland freshwater and brackish wetlands. It is also often seen in paddy fields, swamps or small waterbodies. The sandpiper's diet mainly consists of worms and larvae, but it also takes on small fish, crustaceans and other aquatic insects. It usually feeds alone but during winter and out of breeding season, forages with flocks, even with other species. The Marsh sandpiper often feeds in shallow water, walking steadily and pecking on the surface. Sometimes, it gleans from the vegetation, and probes, jabs or sweeps the bill into the water. It is a winter visitor here.

± 24 CM, FRESHWATER AND BRACKISH WETLANDS

## Wood Sandpiper

### *Tringa glareola* भूरा चौबाहा

Also known as the Spotted sandpiper, the Wood sandpiper is one of the most abundant waders in winter. According to historical records, the 'snippet' could be found in winter about every jheel, village tank, river, inundated ploughed field and marshes. It forages by probing in shallow water or on wet mud, and mainly eats insects and similar small prey. It usually nests on the ground or uses abandoned nests of other birds on trees.

± 20 CM, BANK OF RIVERS, FRESHWATER MARSHES AND PUDDLES

## Green Sandpiper

*Tringa ochropus* हरा चौबाहा

This dark brown sandpiper with a snowy white belly bobs its tail when nervous, but not habitually like the Common sandpiper. It often climbs steeply when flushed and flies quickly with deep wing beats, swooping around a little. Mainly found alone or in small groups, it does not mix with other species. Primarily, the bird feeds on small invertebrates picked off the mud as it works steadily around the edges of a waterbody. The Green sandpiper is migratory to Lucknow.

© Rajesh Panwar

± 23 CM, STREAMS, RIVERS AND FRESHWATER MARSHES

## Common Sandpiper

*Actitis hypoleucos*

The Common sandpiper is a small and graceful solitary bird, often found feeding along the sides of ponds, rivers, streams, canals and even along the seashore. Although well able to swim, dive or wade if the necessity arises, it prefers to feed exactly along the edge of the water, tripping along the margin of sand or mud, just dipping its toes in the water and picking its food from the surface of the shore. It incessantly nods its head and jerks its tail up and down. This sandpiper feeds on insects and their larvae, sandhoppers, freshwater shrimps and other similar small organisms.

© Rajesh Panwar

± 20 CM, STREAMS, LAKES AND FRESHWATER MARSHES

CW LC

# Temminck's Stint

## *Calidris temminckii* टेमिंक पनलवा

This bird breeds mainly in the wet moorland of Scandinavia and Russia and migrates to a variety of wetland habitats across Africa and southern Asia. Found mainly as single or in small groups, they often appear as part of flocks locally. It stays away from other shorebirds, feeding quietly in the marshy and muddy edges in or adjacent to cover. This very small bird has a rather plain plumage (except for the bright marks on the back of breeding adults) and greenish-yellow legs. When in flight, the sides of the tail appear to be bright white, unlike the grey of the little stint.

© Rajesh Panwar

± 14 CM, VEGETATED FRESHWATER WETLANDS, SHALLOW POOLS

LCW | LC

# Ruff

## *Philomachus pugnax* रफ रीव

The Ruff is a medium-sized wading bird and has a distinctive gravy boat appearance, with a small head, long neck, medium-length bill, long legs and a pot-bellied body. It can be spotted in almost any wetland habitat, from reservoirs and fields to coastal mudflats. It feeds by probing and picking for food, often while in shallow water. It is highly gregarious and during migration, travels in large flocks that can contain hundreds or thousands of birds.

© Neeraj Mishra

± 30 CM (M) & 25 CM (F), FRESHWATER WETLANDS & FLOODED FIELDS

LCW | LC

# Pin-tailed Snipe

*Gallinago stenura* सींख पूँछ चाहा

The Pin-tailed snipe is found in every type of marshy and flooded ground where soft mud combines with cover. It is, however, occasionally found in dry grasslands, stubbles or low scrubs. This is due to the fact that the pintail does not have a highly specialised bill like the Common snipe, and therefore feeds less on worms and more on insects, larvae and molluscs. It is a winter visitor.

© Rajesh Panwar

± 26 CM, MARSHES AND PADDY FIELDS

NCW LC

# Common Snipe

*Gallinago gallinago* सामान्य चाहा

The Common snipe is a small, long-beaked bird, found in a variety of habitats, which has both water and some cover. It is mainly nocturnal, but also feeds a good deal in early mornings and evenings. It spends the rest of the day drowsing in the shade of a tuft of grass or rushes. When the weather is particularly hot, it leaves the jheels to take shelter in the cool depths of luxuriant crops or patches of scrub. It feeds on the seeds of marsh plants and small molluscs, but a great portion of its diet consists of minute worms and larvae, obtained by boring into soft mud. The Common snipe is a winter visitor to the city.

© Amit Mishra

± 26 CM, MARSHES AND PADDY STUBBLES

LCW LC

# ROSTRATULIDAE (Painted-snipes)

Painted-snipes are short-legged, long-billed birds similar in shape to the true snipes. All species in this family generally inhabit reedy swamps and marshes, usually in the lowlands. Outside of the breeding season, they generally remain solitary. Painted-snipes are crepuscular and, in some cases, slightly nocturnal in their habits. Mostly omnivorous, they feed on invertebrates and seeds. They also prey on annelid worms, snails, aquatic and marsh insects, and crustaceans. The seeds of grasses such as millet and rice also form a major part of the diet of some of the species.

• Greater Painted-snipe

# Greater Painted-snipe

*Rostratula benghalensis* राजचाहा

± 25 CM, FRESHWATER MARSHES AND SHALLOW, VEGETATED POOLS

LCR | LC

The Greater Painted-snipe is a small, squat bird with a round head, long bills and what looks like a pair of creamy-white spectacles. Its eyes are located higher up on its head, which gives it an all-round vision. A widely distributed bird, it grows in grassy marshes that abound in deep pools and soft muddy patches. Painted-snipe is the most active during the early morning or evening hours and can be heard at close quarters. When it senses any kind of danger, it prefers running for cover to flying off. After a while though, it tends to return to the spot it was flushed from.

The bird feeds on molluscs, insects, crabs and worms. They can be seen wagging their rear end up and down as they do their long, slightly-down curved (at the tips only) bill, probing deeply into the mire. This species is polyandrous, which means one female has many males as partners, and the male incubates eggs and rears chicks. Females are bigger and more brightly coloured than the males.

© Amit Mishra

# JACANIDAE
## (Jacanas)

Jacanas live in a variety of shallow freshwater wetlands with emergent or floating vegetation. Their nests consist of fairly sparse floating mass of vegetation, usually built on the surface of shallow waterbodies. The female bird initially helps with nest-making but later, the rest of the responsibilities, such as incubation, brooding and caring for the chicks, are shouldered by the male bird. The male bird often shelters the young under its wings in case of any danger. Under threat, the chicks may also snorkel whereby they completely submerge themselves in the water with only their bill above the surface to breathe. Insects, molluscs and crustaceans are part of their diet. It has been observed that in some species, at some time, seeds (mostly of water lily) may constitute 20 per cent to 50 per cent of their diet. Jacanas are said to be the water striders of the bird world. Though they cannot walk on water, their long, slender toes and long, splint-like nails, allow them to walk on very flimsy floating vegetation. Not an ardent flier but the bird is capable of flying readily whenever there is a threat. Jacanas spend much of their time away from cover.

- Pheasant-tailed Jacana
- Bronze-winged Jacana

# Pheasant-tailed Jacana

± 30 CM, FRESHWATER WETLANDS WITH VEGETATION AND FLOATING PLANTS

LCR | LC

## *Hydrophasianus chirurgus* पिहो

The Pheasant-tailed jacana is one of the commonest waders. It lives in and around tanks, marshes and lakes, where thickets of reeds, lotus and other floating plants are present. Its long toes and claws allow it to walk easily on those floating plants. This bird resembles the Pond heron in terms of its capacity for startling the unobservant. Standing on submerged weeds in the water, it easily escapes observation until it rises with a sudden startling flash of white wings, flitting away over water until it settles again and becomes invisible once more. Though the bird is capable of swimming, it usually prefers to walk on the vegetation. The female bird is more colourful than the male and is polyandrous.

© Ashish Loya

# Bronze-winged Jacana

± 30 CM, FRESHWATER WETLANDS WITH VEGETATION

CR | LC

*Metopidius indicus* जल पीपी

The Bronze-winged jacana is a common bird of our wetlands. Purely a waterbird, it never frequents rivers but lives exclusively in marshes and swamps, especially those in which the surface of the water is paved and hidden from view by the leaves of lotus, and other floating and emergent vegetation. The elongated toes, and straight and lengthy claws give its feet a snowshoe-like surface, which allows the bird to move about easily over the broad, flat lotus leaves and the flimsiest of weeds. The Bronze-winged jacana feeds on vegetable matter, insects, larvae, molluscs and crustaceans.

# BURHINIDAE

## (Stone-curlew, Stone-plover [Thick-knees])

Birds in this family are strictly ground-dwelling and run swiftly with short, quick steps, neck outstretched and held almost in line with their horizontal body. They inhabit open, dry and stony plains, dotted here and there by scanty bushes and scrub. They are also found on ploughed and fallow land and on the shingly beds of dry streams. They are mostly crepuscular and nocturnal in their habits. These birds are sluggish during the day, resting in the shade of bushes or under a grove of trees. When suspicious or alarmed, they, after scuttling over a short distance, squat low with the body pressed to the ground, head and neck extended in front.

- Great Thick-knee or Great Stone-curlew
- Indian Thick-knee or Indian Stone-curlew

# Indian Thick-knee

± 38 CM, STONY, DRY RIVERBEDS WITH SCRUB AND WET AREAS

LCR | LC

*Burhinus (oedicnemus) indicus* यूरेशियाई करवान

Also known as the Thick-knee or Goggle-eyed plover, the Indian Thick-knee is a ground bird with a thick head and conspicuous round goggle eyes. Almost the size of a partridge, it loves to venture into the dry, stony areas or shingly beds of dry streams. Its colouration allows it the perfect camouflage and makes it look exactly like a diminutive mound of earth, even at close range. Its food consists principally of insects, worms, slugs and small reptiles, and as birds do not have teeth, they swallow small stones and grit for masticating their food.

© Amit Mishra

# RECURVIROSTRIDAE (Stilts and Avocets)

Elegant, and essentially black-and-white wading birds, all the members of this family possess long, thin legs, necks and bills. Avocets have slender, upcurved bills adapted for a sideways sweep across the surface of wet mud or shallow water to find food, whereas stilts have especially long, slender legs with short toes and needle-like bills. Stilts and avocets breed on open ground near water, often in loose colonies. They defend their nesting territories vigorously and with aggressive displays, from any mob of intruders and possible predators, with a great deal of noise. It has been studied that stilt and avocet chicks feed themselves as they are not fed by their parents.

- Black-winged Stilt
- Pied Avocet

# Black-winged Stilt

± 38 CM, FRESHWATER WETLANDS, IRRIGATION TANKS AND SPILLOVERS

**LCR** LC

## *Himantopus himantopus* गजपाँव

The Black-winged stilt is a slender black-and-white bird with long straight beak and absurdly long red legs. Owing to its long legs and long bill, it is able to wade into deeper water unlike most waders, and therefore tap into food resources that are not available to them. It is always found wading in water, picking with its bill from the water surface, often in noisy colonies. When it is in flight, its long pink legs stick out far beyond the tail. It occasionally associates with avocets and godwits (similar long-legged birds), but do not, as a rule, mix with the other waders. Its food consists of seeds of water plants, insects, molluscs and worms.

# Pied Avocet

*Recurvirostra avosetta* कस्या चाहा

± 43 CM, FRESHWATER WETLANDS, POOLS

NCW LC

The Pied avocet is an attractive long-legged, long-beaked wading bird of the muddy shores of shallow lakes and lagoons, including both freshwater and saline waters. It is very easily spotted because of its striking and essentially unmistakable elegant shape, conspicuous black-and-white feathers and upcurved bill. Its diet consists of aquatic insects, small crustaceans and worms. It feeds while wading in shallow water, sweeping its bill side to side. It is an uncommon winter visitor in Lucknow, hence, is not a commonly seen bird in this region.

# CHARADRIIDAE (Plovers and Lapwings)

Plovers occupy diverse habitats and are found from deserts to open savannah to alpine tundra, to even golf courses, lawns and mudflats. They feed mainly on insects, worms and small crustaceans as well as seeds and berries, especially when amassing fat stores for long transoceanic journey. They locate their food by sight and chase after it, running and stopping to eat, then running again.

Lapwings are possessive when it comes to parental care. In most species, the male and the female take care of the nest and the chicks. Chicks are precocial, which means they can feed themselves within 24 hours of hatching. The parents are very protective and engage in an aggressive display to chase off predators. They may even drag one wing along the ground and pretend to be injured in order to draw predators away from their nests. Essentially a ground-nesting species, they are commonly found near water.

- Little-ringed Plover
- Kentish Plover
- Red-wattled Lapwing
- Yellow-wattled Lapwing
- River Lapwing
- Grey-headed Lapwing
- White-tailed Lapwing

# Little-ringed Plover

*Charadrius dubius* जीरा बाटन

The Little-ringed Plover is a delicately built bird with conspicuous bright yellow eye rings. When in flight, narrow indistinct white stripes become visible on its wings. It prefers to remain on the ground, spending most of its time seeking food. It can be seen walking with dainty steps and little short runs, and bobbing down with a curious characteristic movement to pick up food. When approached, it flies rapidly, low over the ground. It has a curious habit; when foraging for food in soft, wet mud, it drums its toes in a rapid vibratory motion in order to dislodge insects, sandhoppers and tiny crabs lurking in their burrows.

± 16 CM, FRESHWATER WETLANDS AND MUDBANKS OF RIVERS

LCR | LC

# Kentish Plover

*Charadrius alexandrinus* कालरवाला बाटन

The Kentish plover is a small and stocky shorebird, found in multiple habitats—from the shore of saline lakes, marshes to sand dunes in deserts. It is a territorial bird, known to protect its territory. This act of protection also functions as courtship display to attract the female bird. Parents actively defend their nest territories from predators by chasing, fighting or posturing them. When faced with predators in close proximity to the nest, the Kentish plovers quickly run away from the nest and try to distract the predators by diverting their focus, luring the danger away from the nest. This bird is a winter visitor to this region.

© Rajesh Panwar

± 16 CM, BANK OF FRESHWATER WETLANDS, SANDY SHORES

LCW | LC

# Red-wattled Lapwing

± 35 CM, OPEN FLAT GROUND USUALLY NEAR WATER AND URBAN ENVIRONS

CR LC

*Vanellus indicus* शरारि टिटहरी

A very common bird of the Indian plains, the Red-wattled lapwing is known for its loud alarm call that sounds like the words 'did-he-do-it'. It haunts open country, ploughed fields and grazing lands, and is almost invariably present on the margins and beds of jheels and spillovers when the water has recently receded. It spends its time running about on the ground in short spurts.

The bird's diet consists of insects, grubs and molluscs. It catches the insects in a typical plover-like manner: running a short distance and picking up food from the ground.

# Yellow-wattled Lapwing

*Vanellus malabaricus* जर्द टिटहरी

± 27 CM, DRY STUBBLES, FALLOW FIELDS AND DRY OPEN COUNTRY

NCR LC

Yet another common terrestrial species of the Indian plains, the Yellow-wattled lapwing inhabits more or less the same type of open habitats—plains, wastes and fallow land—as its cousin, the Red-wattled lapwing. But it prefers drier habitats and is less dependent upon the neighbouring water resources. This lapwing's food consists of beetles, termites and other invertebrates, which are picked from the ground.

# River Lapwing

*Vanellus duvaucelii* जल टिटहरी

The River lapwing is an attractive shorebird with a black crest, crown, face and throat. The adult male is slightly larger than the female. Strictly terrestrial, the bird prominently inhabits wide, slow rivers with sand or gravel bars and islands. It is fairly common in this area. It has sedentary habits and nests on shingle and sandbanks. It feeds on insects, worms, crustaceans and molluscs in sandy banks, wet grasslands and farmlands.

± 32 CM, SAND OR SHINGLE BANKS OF RIVERS AND MARSHES

LCR LC

# Grey-headed Lapwing

*Vanellus cinereus* स्लेटी सिर टिटहरी

As the name suggests, the Grey-headed lapwing is a medium-sized bird with a grey head, neck and breast. It is not as common as its cousins. Though, during the winter months, it is seen in small groups or pairs in the open countryside and soggy beds of wetlands. It forages in shallow water and feeds on insects, worms and molluscs.

© Amit Mishra

± 35 CM, RIVERBANKS, MARSHES AND WET FIELDS

LCW LC

# GLAREOLIDAE (Coursers and Pratincoles)

This is a family of strictly terrestrial birds. Coursers frequent dry and stony areas or grasslands. While pratincoles prefer similar habitats, they need to be near water. These birds have arched and pointed bills, wide gapes and long, pointed wings. Coursers are long-legged and feed on the ground while with shorter legs, pratincoles catch most of their prey in the air.

- Indian Courser
- Small Pratincole

# Small Pratincole

± 18 CM, SANDY BANKS OF RIVERS OR LAKE AND SHINGLE BANKS

NCR | LC

*Glareola lactea* छोटी धोबैचा

The Small pratincole is a sandy-grey bird and is found about the sandbanks of larger and more placid rivers. It leaves these sites, only occasionally, in the evening, for open lakes in the vicinity. It has long and pointed wings and very short legs. It is crepuscular when it comes to foraging activities. Invariably found in large colonies, which are social throughout their lives, this bird breeds in large numbers. It feeds as part of large flocks, which skim about the surface of rivers and lakes, catching insects on the wing. The Small pratincole eats beetles, bugs, termites, flies and other insects. It also chases insects across sandy ground. This pratincole is not a common bird in Lucknow.

# LARIDAE (Gulls)

Gulls are usually grey or white, often with black markings on the head or wings. Their size ranges from medium to large. Gulls are generalist feeders. As they are ground-nesting carnivores, they take live food or scavenge opportunistically. They feed on fish, and marine and freshwater invertebrates, both alive and dead. Most gull species are migratory, with the birds moving to warmer habitats during winter.

- Brown-headed Gull
- Black-headed Gull
- Caspian Gull
- Pallas's Gull

© Amit Mishra

## Brown-headed Gull

*Chroicocephalus brunnicephalus* सामान्य धोमरा

One of the common seagulls in most areas, the Brown-headed gull is found in a variety of habitats, from large rivers and streams to wild wetlands and seacoasts. It is usually seen in flocks consisting of hundreds, sometimes, thousands of members. The gull's plumage is mostly white, except towards the tip of the wings, which is black. This bird is a bold and opportunist feeder, which scavenges in towns or catches invertebrates in ploughed fields with equal relish. The Brown-headed gull is a winter visitor to Lucknow, and migrates from the upper reaches of the Himalayas—its breeding ground.

± 42 CM, LARGE INLAND LAKES AND SLOW-MOVING RIVERS

NCW | LC

## Black-headed Gull

*Chroicocephalus ridibundus* कालशीर्ष धोमरा

A fairly small sized gull, easily recognised by the dark spot behind its ear and with red bill and legs. In winter, the head is not black. It becomes black during the breeding season. The Black-headed gull inhabits a variety of habitats, from duck ponds and farm fields to large rivers and sea coasts. Like most gulls, it is highly gregarious in winter, when not breeding, especially when feeding or while roosting in the evenings. It eats insects, fish, seeds, worms, scraps, and carrion as well as invertebrates. During winter months, this species is spotted in a few patches of the Gomti River, on the outer limits of the main city.

± 38 CM, LARGE INLAND LAKES AND RIVERS

NCW | LC

# Pallas's Gull

*Ichthyaetus ichthyaetus* बड़ा धोमरा

± 68 CM, LARGE INLAND LAKES AND RIVERS

NCW LC

Also known as the Great Black-headed gull, it is a widespread winter visitor. It is a large, powerful gull of freshwater, saline and brackish waterbodies. The eye crescents and flashy white rumps help to distinguish them in winter. Its size also makes them distinct from other smaller dark-headed gulls. Mostly solitary or seen in small flocks, this gull stays leisurely on sandy or shallow part of a river or at the water's edge, waiting for its prey. In India, most gulls do not have dark head. The bird is not a common winter visitor in Lucknow.

# STERNIDAE (Terns)

Also known as Sea swallows, terns are a family of smaller, slimmer and daintily-built birds. They possess long, forked tail, narrow wings, long bill and relatively short legs. They never perch on trees, nor do they settle on the water or swim generally. Despite having webbed feet, they rarely swim, rather scout over water, in buoyant flight, with the beak pointing down. Most terns hunt fish by hovering over the waterbody before diving in. This particular technique is specific to this family and can help identify the species at a distance.

- Little Tern
- Black-bellied Tern
- River Tern
- Whiskered Tern

# River Tern

*Sterna aurantia* जल कुररी

± 45 CM, LARGE INLAND LAKES AND RIVERS

NCR | LC

A graceful grey-and-white bird with long pointed wings and a forked tail. The River tern is equal to the size of pigeon but is a much slimmer bird. Mostly a river bird, it also visits lakes and big marshes where it can be seen circling over the surface of the water and looking for fish, during the day. It captures a small fish by dropping perpendicularly into the water and then eats its prey on the wing, invariably swallowing the head first.

## Black-bellied Tern

*Sterna acuticauda* कलपेटी कुररी

As the name suggests, it is a bird with a black belly (during the breeding season), forked tail, and yellow or orange bill and feet. The habits of the Black-bellied tern are very similar to those of the common River tern. The Black-bellied tern can often be found in the company of the latter. This bird feeds on insects and small fish, skimming over the surface of the water and ground to pick them up. It also plunges obliquely into the water to feed on crustaceans, tadpoles and fish.

± 33 CM, LARGE INLAND LAKES AND RIVERS

**NCR** Endangered

## Whiskered Tern

*Chlidonias hybrida* मुच्छल कुररी

A graceful looking whitish bird, the Whiskered tern is seen in the winter months with its off-black cap and white belly as its non-breeding plumage. It feeds in the company of other similar birds, over water or paddy fields, delicately capturing insects. It is interesting to watch the bird feeds on the wing in a most methodical manner. Dragon-flies and their larvae constitute the staple food of this bird, but water beetles and other aquatic insects are eaten as well. The Whiskered tern breeds in high altitude regions of India, and is a winter visitor to Lucknow.

© Amit Mishra

± 24 CM, INDIAN LAKES AND RIVERS

**NCW** LC

# ACCIPITRIDAE (Raptors)
## (Hawks, Kites, Vultures, Eagles and Buzzards)

The word raptor is derived from the Latin word *rapere* and it means 'to seize or capture'. This is a common attribute of the birds of this family. Raptors belong to one of the largest family of birds. Many well-known birds, such as hawks, eagles, kites and harriers are included in this group. Raptors, or birds of prey, have a hooked beak, excellent eyesight, sharp talons, and strong legs and feet for tearing its prey's flesh. A raptor's beak is one feature used to set them apart from other birds. Most birds of prey will have three toes pointing forward and one pointing backwards. These toes hold their prey in an extremely powerful grip, literally crushing it to death. Raptors are believed to have the keenest eyesight in nature because of the size of the eyeball and the eye muscles designed for rapid focus.

- Shikra
- Indian Spotted Eagle
- Greater Spotted Eagle
- Oriental Honey Buzzard
- Tawny Eagle
- Imperial Eagle
- Crested Serpent Eagle
- Eurasian Sparrowhawk
- Pallas's Fish Eagle
- Steppe Eagle
- Booted Eagle
- Bonelli's Eagle
- Crested Hawk-eagle
- White-eyed Buzzard
- Short-toed Snake Eagle
- Long-legged Buzzard
- Eurasian Marsh Harrier
- Pallid Harrier

# Short-toed Snake Eagle

± 65 CM, OPEN COUNTRY, SCRUB-COVERED HILLS

NCR | LC

*Circaetus gallicus* साँपमार चील

Also known simply as the Short-toed eagle, this bird is a medium-sized bird of prey and a large, slightly ungainly raptor with long and broad wings, short tail, and a conspicuously big head. It is found in open cultivated plains, arid stony deciduous scrub areas and foothills and semi-desert areas. It requires trees for nesting, and open habitats, such as cultivated lands and grasslands, for foraging. Known as an accomplished flyer, it spends more time on the wing than most members of its genus do. It hunts over open areas and its prey is mostly reptiles, mainly snakes and also some lizards, Sometimes, they become entangled with larger snakes and engage in battle on the ground.

# Crested Serpent Eagle

*Spilornis cheela* डोगरा चील

The Crested Serpent eagle is a widely distributed bird. The full crest, broad white bar in the tail, combined with the noisy whistling calls, renders this eagle easier than most to identify. This handsome eagle is found in well-wooded and well-watered country. As the name suggests, its food consists chiefly of snakes, lizards, frogs and insects. The claws are usually dirty with mud, indicating how large a portion of the food is procured from paddy fields and lakes. It prefers flying over forests and well-wooded ravines to flying over barren and open ground. It often flies up to a great height, travelling fast or soaring in great circles. The Crested Serpent eagle is a fairly common bird in the city.

± 72 CM, FORESTS AND WELL-WOODED COUNTRY

**LCR** LC

# Indian Spotted Eagle

*Aquila hastata* देसी चित्रा उकाब

A stocky, medium-sized eagle with short, broad wings and a rather short tail, the adult bird is essentially brown and requires a closer look for identification. The Indian Spotted eagle is a powerful predator that seizes its prey—usually mammals—from the ground whilst quartering over areas within or near forests. This tree-nesting bird also preys on frogs and birds.

± 65 CM, WOODED-AREAS INTERSPERSED WITH CULTIVATION IN LOWLANDS

**NCR** Vulnerable

# Shikra

## *Accipiter badius* शिकरा

± 34 CM, WELL-WOODED OPEN COUNTRY AND GARDENS

CR LC

A small, stout hawk with fierce orange eye, Shikra is one of the commonest and best-known hawks in India. It is found in almost all kinds of habitats, but prefers cultivated tracts with plenty of large trees. It spends most of its time sitting up in the leafy branches of large trees. The tactics it employs in capturing prey are mainly those of surprise. From its perch, hidden well by some leafy tree, it keeps a sharp lookout for lizards, rats, frogs, locusts and other small animals. Its usual call notes are similar to those of the Black drongo, but on a higher scale.

# Oriental Honey Buzzard

± 60 CM, WELL-WOODED COUNTRY, LARGE COMPOUNDS AND CULTIVATION

CR | LC

*Pernis ptilorhynchus* शाहुतेला

The Oriental Honey buzzard, also known as the Crested Honey buzzard, is a medium-sized bird of prey. It feeds on bees, their larvae, wasps and cicadas. It has also been observed eating bits of honeycomb and honey. Solitary or in pairs, this buzzard can be seen either perched on forest trees or flying. It is also known to often enter villages and outskirts of small towns.

# Tawny Eagle

## *Aquila rapax* छोटा जुमिज उकाब

A large brown or blackish-brown bird, the Tawny eagle has a rather fierce appearance—a flat head, sharp claws and sharply-hooked beak. It is particularly a bird of somewhat sandy plains with a moderate amount of tree growth.

The bird is commonly found in this region and can be easily identified by its round tail. The Tawny eagle is a fine lordly-looking bird. It hunts hares and large birds, and even chases and robs falcons and hawks of their booty. Its diet includes frogs, lizards and snakes.

© Rajesh Panwar

± 70 CM, OPEN COUNTRY AND CULTIVATED TRACTS NEAR VILLAGES

LCW | LC

# Booted Eagle

## *Hieraaetus pennatus* गिलहरीमार बाज़

The bird's name comes from its feathered legs (boots), prominent when perched. The Booted eagle is a comparatively small bird of prey. It is found in forested country with open patches, often in hilly areas, where it frequently soars with wings slightly pushed forward. It hunts in clearings. Besides rodents, rabbits and lizards, it feeds on small- to medium-sized birds.

© Rajesh Panwar

± 52 CM, GROVES AROUND CULTIVATION AND VILLAGES

LCW | LC

# Steppe Eagle

*Aquila nipalensis* रगड़ उकाब

± 80 CM, OPEN COUNTRY AND RIVER BEDS

**LCW** LC

The Steppe eagle is a large, dark-brown bird of prey. It prefers open areas including farmlands, steppe lands, meadows and open wooded areas. Its diet is largely fresh carrion of all kinds. It also hunts rodents and other small mammals up to the size of a hare, and birds up to the size of partridges. This eagle is also known to steal food from other raptors. Like the other species of the family, the Steppe eagle has a crop in its throat, allowing it to store food for several hours before being moved to the stomach.

© Dr Vivek Banerjee

# White-eyed Buzzard

*Butastur teesa* टीसा

± 42 CM, DRY OPEN COUNTRY

LCR | LC

The White-eyed buzzard is a medium-sized brown hawk, easily identified by its white eyes and the three dark stripes on its white throat. It prefers dry open scrublands, deciduous forests and cultivated country. It can be seen sitting on telegraph posts, trees or low bushes, from which it occasionally descends to the ground to capture food. Its diet consists of locusts, grasshoppers, crickets and other insects as well as small rodents. In fact, it is an effective pest controller.

In Lucknow, one can spot the bird in abandoned areas of railway yards, where grass is generally long and full of grasshoppers, lizards, rats and mice.

© Amit Mishra

# Long-legged Buzzard

*Buteo rufinus* लमटंगा चूहामार

± 60 CM, DRY OPEN COUNTRY

LCW LC

This fine buzzard is very common in the wide plains of northwest India, specifically cultivated lands and marshy ground. The Long-legged buzzard is a rather sluggish bird and can be spotted sitting limply on the ground or on a tree. Its flight is slow and heavy, but it soars easily high above the ground for long periods, moving in great spirals. It often hunts from a prominent perch, or sitting on the ground in steppe or desert country, sometimes, in wooded areas, but always near big open spaces.

© Rajesh Panwar

## Pied Harrier

± 45 CM, OPEN GRASSLAND AND CULTIVATION

NCW SO

*Circus melanoleucos* अबलक पत्तई

A fairly small bird of prey, it is known for its elegant and spectacular appearance. It is migratory, and in winter months, often seen hunting above rice paddies and wetlands near cultivation. In Lucknow, a solitary bird was seen in the open field on the outskirts. It is an uncommon bird in Lucknow and no confirmed records are available.

© Clement Francis

© Amit Mishra

# VULTURES

Historically abundant in Lucknow, vultures play a significant role in the ecology. They are also called the masters of the sky on account of their strength. In a detailed account of the birds of the Lucknow division, it was stated that the white-backed vulture is common in all seasons. It breeds from November till the end of March, making its nest on tall trees, as high as possible. In the vicinity of Lucknow, there are breeding sites where at least 50 or 60 such nest may be found, two or three on the same tree. In the year 1990, signs of decline of vultures were recorded. The most affected species were gyps, which have been reduced to countable numbers today. Most of the species of the family stay away from human habitations. The Long-hilled vulture always breeds on high cliffs, while White-backed vulture is content to build its nest on any tree, high enough to bear the weight of the nest. Mango or fig trees are the preferred nesting sites in their case. Another noticeable and interesting thing is that all the other birds of prey carry food with their feet, but it is impossible for vultures because they are incapable of swooping and cannot even rise off the ground without running. However, once in the air, no other bird can match the way they fly and glide in the sky. Collectively, for hours together, they can be seen sailing in circles, or rather in spirals, without the slightest movement of their wings.

- White-rumped Vulture
- Indian Vulture
- Egyptian Vulture
- Himalayan Griffon
- Red-headed Vulture

# White-rumped or White-backed Vulture

*Gyps bengalensis* चमर गिद्द

± 80 CM, TREETOPS, BUILDINGS, CITIES, TOWNS AND VILLAGES

CR | LC

Earlier known as the Bengal vulture, it is a smoky-black bird with a band of white extending nearly the whole length of each wing on the underside. This band is broken by its dark body and helps identify the bird at a glance. Known as one of the finest scavengers, it feeds mostly on the ground, but roosts and nests in trees and cliffs, and spend much of their time soaring on wind currents searching for carrion. Once a common bird in most of the country—often found in cities, towns and villages, near human habitations—its numbers have now declined to a critical level. The White-rumped vulture is now categorised as critically endangered and is facing imminent extinction.

# Egyptian Vulture

## *Neophron percnopterus* सफेद गिद्द

± 70 CM, OPEN COUNTRYSIDE AND CULTIVATION

LCR EN

The Egyptian vulture is a pale, medium-sized bird with a bare, solemn-looking yellow face and is considerably smaller than those vultures reported in Lucknow. An inhabitant of open or semi-open areas, this bird mostly nests on cliffs and less frequently on trees. It is opportunistic and eats a variety of seeds. Its diet consists of mainly carrion but also young birds, small mammals, fish, eggs and even rotting fruits. It can fly up to 80 kilometres per day in search of food. Being a small bird, it waits for food left by larger species. Its thin beak is perfectly adapted to catch the small pieces of leftover meat on carcasses.

Egyptian Vulture (sub-adult)

Egyptian Vulture (adult)

# KITES

We have three species of kites in Lucknow: the Black kite, the Black-eared kite and the Black-shouldered kite. Kites are the raptors that spend a great amount of time soaring in the sky. They are generally smaller than hawks and eagles. Kites play a crucial role as a rodent controller because of their scavenging abilities.

- Black Kite
- Black-eared Kite
- Black-winged/shouldered Kite

# Black Kite

## *Milvus migrans* सामान्य चील

Also known as the Common Pariah kite, the Black kite is one of the most familiar birds of India. It is a fearless scavenger, and more or less spends its whole life either robbing man of food that he would fain keep or scavenging the offal that has been thrown away. It frequents every bazaar and village, sitting on the buildings and trees, awaiting something worthy of its attention, or patrolling the ground with sweeping easy flight in wide circles, in search of food. The call of the Black kite is a shrill, mewing, long-drawn squeal, almost musical, and is most frequently heard during the breeding season.

± 64 CM, AROUND CITIES, TOWNS AND VILLAGES

CR | LC

# Black-eared Kite

## *Milvus (migrans) lineatus* काली चील

It is a large diurnal raptor with dark ear-coverts and shallow forked tail. Unlike others in its family, this kite is an opportunistic hunter and is more likely to scavenge. It spends a lot of time soaring and gliding in thermals in search of food. Its angled wing and distinctive forked tail makes it easy to identify the bird. It is mostly migratory, winter visitor to this region.

± 65 CM, OPEN COUNTRY, AROUND HUMAN HABITATIONS AND WATERBODIES

LCR | LC

# Black-winged/ shouldered Kite

## *Elanus caeruleus* कपासी चील

± 34 CM, OPEN COUNTRY INTERSPERSED WITH CULTIVATION OR SCATTERED TREES

**LCR** LC

It is a fairly small and distinctive falcon-like kite. This kite inhabits well-wooded country and cultivated lands. Although somewhat crepuscular, and more active in the early mornings and just before dusk, the bird may nevertheless be seen hunting sluggishly throughout the day. It keeps to a favoured locality and perches on the same pole or treetop, day after day. It has varied flight styles: hovering like a kestrel, or gliding like a harrier with deep wing beats and raised wings. Its food consists of locusts, crickets and other insects, lizards, rats and mice. It also consumes sickly or wounded birds.

# PANDIONIDAE

## Osprey

± 56 CM, LAKES, RIVERS AND SHALLOW WETLANDS

LCW | LC

*Pandion haliaetus* मछलीमार

The Osprey is also known as the Fish eagle, the River hawk or the Fish hawk. With a white head and neck, black stripes through eyes and a short tail, it is pretty easy to identify the bird. It is a winter visitor to Uttar Pradesh and is found near wetlands, hovering over water surface when fishing. It is also found in a wide variety of habitats, but proximity to water is a must.

The Osprey feeds on fish captured with their talons by flying low over the water, or by snatching from the surface in shallow water.

# FALCONIDAE (Falcons)

Falcons are consummate hunters of the avian world—able to spot, chase and kill prey quietly and efficiently. They are widely distributed around the world. Adult falcons have thin, tapered wings, which enable them to fly at high speed and change direction rapidly. Fledgeling falcons, in their first year of flying, have longer flight feathers, which make their configuration more like that of a general-purpose bird, such as a broad-wing. This makes flying easier while learning the exceptional skills required to be effective hunters as adults. All these birds kill with their beaks, using a 'tooth' on the side of their beaks, unlike the hawks, eagles, and other birds of prey of the accipitradae family, which use their feet.

# Eurasian or Common Kestrel

± 35 CM, CULTIVATION, GRASSLANDS AND SEMI-DESERTS

LCW LC

*Falco tinnunculus* सामान्य खेरमुतिया

A small falcon with pointed wings and rather long, fan-shaped tail, this kestrel is necessarily a bird of open country and spends most of its time hunting over cultivated tracts, bare hillsides and open grassy plains. It perches on rocks or trees and thence watches for food, its head incessantly turning and bobbing. Once it spots anything of interest, it silently leaves the perch and flies with half-bent wings towards the ground, and desperately dashes towards the object of its attention. The Eurasian kestrel feeds on lizards, grasshoppers and mice, which it takes from the ground. Occasionally, it also catches small birds. This winter visitor to Lucknow is a graceful bird, and it is a pleasure to observe its movements.

© Rajesh Panwar

# Peregrine Falcon

*Falco peregrinus* शाहीन

± 50 CM, AROUND LAKES, RIVERS AND MARSHES

This large and powerful raptor feeds mainly on birds captured in flight. The Peregrine falcon has been a symbol of speed and power for centuries. They were a favourite of the ancient Egyptians and Chinese who practised falconry as early 2000 BCE. It is one of the swiftest and deadliest of the birds of prey. Known for swooping on its prey at speeds of up to 300 km/h, it preys almost exclusively on birds, mostly doves and pigeons.

© Rajesh Panwar

# Laggar Falcon

± 45 CM, ARID OPEN COUNTRY AND CULTIVATION

LCW LC

*Falco jugger* लग्गर

The Laggar is one of our commonest falcons. It frequents dry, open scrub country, the outskirts of thin jungles and cultivated lands, but avoids humid forest tracts. A pair frequently take up their quarters within the limits of a town, using a tower or church-spire as foraging base, whence they prey on the urban pigeon population. In addition to small birds, their diet consists of field rats, lizards, locusts, dragonflies and the like. The Laggar used to be trained for hunting birds like partridges, pond-herons, crows and floricans, but with the decline in the vogue of falconry, these birds are now seldom trained.

© Rajesh Panwar

# PODICIPEDIDAE (Grebes)

Grebes are small- to medium-sized foot-propelled diving birds with round bodies and tiny tails. They are expert swimmers and divers, but are unable to walk on dry land. They swim by simultaneously spreading out their feet and bringing them inward, with the webbing expanded to produce the forward thrust in much the same way as frogs. They feed largely on fish, besides small invertebrates and crustaceans.

- Little Grebe
- Great Crested Grebe

# Little Grebe

*Tachybaptus ruficollis* छोटा डूबडुबी

± 28 CM, OPEN WATER, LAKES, PONDS AND VILLAGE TANKS

CR | LC

The Little grebe or Dabchick is the smallest of the true waterbirds of India. It is found in lakes, marshes and tanks, swimming low in the water and disappearing under it at the smallest provocation. Rather compact, with rounded head, puffy rear end, it is seen either alone or in small loose flocks. Much of its food in the way of small fishes is acquired underwater, for it dives well and can swim far beneath the surface. It also feeds on the surface, sometimes on vegetable matter, small molluscs and water insects.

# Great Crested Grebe

± 50 CM, OPEN WATER, LAKES AND RESERVOIRS

**LCW** LC

*Podiceps cristatus* शिवा डूबडुबी

Large, elegant, and long-necked, the Great Crested grebe is fairly common in and around lakes, reservoirs, and along larger rivers, mainly lined by reeds, where it builds a floating nest platform. Except during the breeding season, it is mostly a solitary bird. Its diet consists mainly of fish but also includes insects, crustaceans and invertebrate larvae. It catches its prey by diving under the surface of the water. This grebe forages the most during dawn and dusk, possibly because this is when its prey is close to the surface. This makes the fish easier to detect visually and also reduce the diving distance. The Great Crested grebe is a winter visitor to this region.

# ANHINGIDAE (Darter)

## Darter

± 95 CM, LAKES, PONDS AND RESERVOIRS

CR NT

*Anhinga melanogaster* बानवे

The Darter has a long, thin neck, which gives it a snake-like appearance when it swims with its body submerged, giving it the name Snake-bird. It is a bird of freshwater rivers, lakes or marshes, the only requisite being that the water should be deep enough for it to swim and dive in. The Darter has completely webbed feet and short legs, set far back on the body. Its plumage is somewhat permeable, like that of cormorants, and it spreads its wings to dry after diving.

# PHALACROCORACIDAE (Cormorant and Shags)

Cormorants are metallic-black in colour and commonly found around waterbodies. They are better known as a fish-eating and colonial-nesting waterbirds. The prominent physical features of these birds are its slender bill hooked at the tip, short legs, large and webbed feet. Both sexes are fairly identical in appearance.

- Little Cormorant
- Indian Shag or Cormorant
- Great Cormorant

# Great Cormorant

*Phalacrocorax carbo* बड़ा पनकौआ

± 95 CM, LARGE- OR MEDIUM-SIZED WETLANDS, RESERVOIRS, RIVERS AND LAKES

CR | LC

One of the commonest species of cormorant, the Great cormorant is also the largest bird in the family and has a white patch on its throat and a long tail. It is often spotted standing on rocks or pilings alongside water. This cormorant dives frequently to feed on fish. Found in a variety of water bodies, from the slow-moving stretch of large rivers to marshes to seasonal ponds, it is always found in small to large groups, depending upon the availability of food in the area it inhabits. It is a common bird of Lucknow.

# Indian Cormorant/Shag

*Phalacrocorax fuscicollis* देसी पनकौआ

The Indian cormorant is a medium-sized bird with a long tail and thin bill. This bird can be identified by its blue eye, small head with a sloping forehead and a long, narrow bill ending in a hooked tip. Often seen standing with its wings held out to dry, this cormorant fishes gregariously in inland rivers or large wetlands.

± 63 CM, LARGE WETLANDS, RESERVOIRS, RIVERS AND LAKES

# Little Cormorant

*Phalacrocorax niger* छोटा पनकौआ

The Little cormorant is completely black, duck-like waterbird with a distinctive flattish head and a bill that is sharply hooked at the tip. The smallest of the cormorants found in the city, this bird is frequently seen swimming with its body submerged in the water, and the head and the neck pointing upwards. Often, the bird suddenly disappears underwater to catch fish. A common wetland bird, it perches upright on a rock with outstretched wings in order to dry.

± 50 CM, LAKES, VILLAGE PONDS AND RESERVOIRS

LCR LC

# ARDEIDAE (Herons, Egrets and Bitterns)

Herons are medium- to large-sized birds with long legs, neck and dagger-like beak. Usually solitary, they also turn gregarious with the change in season. They are known for nesting communally in mixed colonies called heronries. They mostly feed on fish, frogs and other aquatic insects in shallow waters or on margins of wetlands.

Most egrets have white plumage and develop long ornamental nuptial plumes for the breeding season. Their habits are generally like those of other herons, but some perform elaborate mating displays involving the plumes. The name Egret, or Aigrette, is also used to refer to these plumes; they are highly prized as ornaments in oriental ceremonial dresses and were formerly used in the western millinery trade. The plume trade is now totally banned in India. It is one of the most familiar birds in Lucknow.

Bitterns are the thickset herons with a bright, pale, buffy-brown plumage and a short neck. They usually frequent reed beds and similar marshy areas. They feed on amphibians, reptiles, insects and fish. They are secretive birds, very difficult to spot, as they move silently through reeds looking for fish.

- Indian Pond Heron
- Black-crowned Night Heron
- Grey Heron
- Purple Heron
- Striated Heron
- Little Egret
- Great Egret
- Intermediate Egret
- Cattle Egret
- Yellow Bittern
- Cinnamon Bittern
- Black Bittern

# Indian Pond Heron

± 44 CM, BOTH URBAN AND VILLAGE PONDS AND DITCHES

CR | LC

## *Ardeola grayii* अंधा बगला

Also known as the Paddy bird, it is a small heron that is common in most aquatic habitats across Lucknow. The bird prefers shallow, static or non-flowing wetlands, big or small. Although typically solitary, large numbers often gather where food is plentiful. It is prone to local seasonal movements and vagrancy. The Indian Pond heron feeds chiefly on frogs, crabs, small fishes, insects and other miscellaneous life forms in or near waterbodies. No puddle is too small, no water too dirty for its attention.

# Black-crowned Night Heron

*Nycticorax nycticorax* वाक बगला

± 64 CM, VEGETATION ADJOINING MARSHES, PONDS AND LAKES

LCR | LC

The Night heron is a small, heavy heron, largely nocturnal in its habits. It sleeps through the day under thick trees. It is short-necked, short-legged and stout bird and usually nests in colonies, on platforms of sticks among a group of trees, or on the ground in protected locations, such as islands or waterbodies, surrounded by thorny plants. It is dependent on water. The Night heron stands still at the water's edge, waiting to ambush its prey, mainly at night. Small fish, crustaceans, frogs, aquatic insects and small mammals are its preferred food.

# Grey Heron

## *Ardea cinerea* स्लेटी अंजन

The Grey heron is a lanky bird of wet habitats and is easily recognised when it stands stock-still in the shallow waters of lakes, rivers and ponds, patiently waiting for fish that flit about below the surface. It is essentially a solitary bird. Sometimes, it wades in shallow water with slow, deliberate pace and an outstretched neck.
It feeds on small mammals, birds, molluscs, insects and crustaceans, but its diet mainly consists of fish. It is also seen in gardens with ornamental ponds, looking for an easy meal.

± 96 CM, WELL-VEGETATED MARSHES, PONDS, LAKES AND RIVERBANKS

**LCR** LC

# Purple Heron

## *Ardea purpurea* नरी अंजन

The Purple heron is a common bird of our wetlands and prefers wet areas with substantial vegetation. It is interesting to see the bird feed in shallow water, waiting motionless for its prey and spearing it with its long, pointed and powerful bill. It is a shy and solitary hunter.

© Amit Mishra

± 88 CM, WELL-VEGETATED MARSHES, PONDS AND LAKES

**LCR** LC

# Little Egret

## *Egretta garzetta* करछिया बगला

A long-legged, long-necked, white bird, the Little egret is generally found throughout the country wherever water is plentiful. Paddy fields, marshes and tanks, rivers and creeks, and even irrigated fields and the neighbourhood of canals are all frequented by the bird. During the breeding season, the adult bird sports an orange-buff on head, neck and mantle. It is a common resident bird and can be observed in or near wetlands or grasslands, often in the company of livestock, generally in parties. Their food mostly consists of fish and frogs, but lizards, worms, grasshoppers, locusts, aquatic insects, freshwater molluscs and crustaceans are also eaten.

± 63 CM, RIVER, MARSHES, PONDS AND PADDY FIELDS

CR | LC

# Great Egret

## *Casmerodius albus* मलंग बगला

The Great egret is a large, pure-white heron with a yellow, dagger-like bill and long, black legs. It forages in shallow wetlands by slowly stalking its prey. It walks with its neck extended and wings held close. When disturbed, and at breeding colonies, it often produces a loud croaking 'cuk cuk cuk' and high-pitched squawks. It feeds in shallow water or drier habitats, mainly on fish, frogs, small mammals and, occasionally, small reptiles and insects, spearing them with its long, sharp bill.

± 100 CM, RIVER, MARSHES, WELL-VEGETATED POOLS

LCR | LC

# Cattle Egret

± 52 CM, DAMP GRASSLANDS, GRASS BANKS OF VILLAGE TANKS AND PADDY FIELDS

CR | LC

*Bubulcus ibis* गाय बगला

The Cattle egret is a slender, white bird with a long neck and a stout yellow bill. One can spot this bird in small or large groups, wherever cattle commonly graze. It sometimes perches on the backs of cattle animals, but more generally, stalks round their legs. It also performs a definite service by ridding their skins of leeches, ticks and other parasites. It is also seen in agriculture fields, catching insect and small vertebrate prey, disturbed by the moving tractors. Its feeding habitats include seasonally inundated grasslands, pastures, farmlands, wetlands and rice paddies. It nests in colonies, usually near waterbodies, and often with other wading birds.

# Black Bittern

*Dupetor flavicollis* काली बगली

± 58 CM, WETLAND EDGES WITH REEDS AND SUBMERGED BUSHES

NCR | LC

The Black bittern prefers wetland habitats with dense fringe vegetation. It is also found in reed beds alongside shallow wetlands like ponds, lakes, streams and marshes. Fish constitute most of the bird's diet, besides amphibians and small vertebrates. The species has a characteristic booming call that is mainly heard during the breeding season, both during the day and at night.

# Chestnut or Cinnamon Bittern

± 38 CM, DAMP GRASSLANDS, GRASS BANKS OF VILLAGE TANKS AND PADDY FIELDS

LCR LC

*Ixobrychus cinnamomeus* लाल बगली

It is a miniature heron with a rich tawny-chestnut colour, that separates the Chestnut bittern from the other birds of the family. Like other bitterns, it prefers reed beds and dense vegetation on the edges of open ponds or marshes. This nocturnal bird hides in the dense cover of reed beds, swamps or rice fields during the day, and by night, they fly out to fish in more open places. It also feeds on frogs, worms and various water insects and larvae. This bird can be spotted in open, seasonal wetlands and areas with sufficient cover, in the outskirts of Lucknow.

© Amit Mishra

# THRESKIORNITHIDAE (Ibis and Spoonbill)

These medium and large wading, terrestrial birds have distinctive shapes and a unique long, thin and decurved bill—broad and flat. They are strong fliers and, rather surprisingly, given their size and weight, very capable soarers. Distributed almost worldwide, they are found near almost any area of standing or slow-flowing freshwater or brackish waterbodies. Ibises are found in drier areas, including landfills. Nesting is colonial, more often in small groups or singly, in trees overhanging water.

- Black-headed Ibis
- Red-naped Ibis
- Glossy Ibis
- Eurasian Spoonbill

# Black-headed Ibis

*Threskiornis melanocephalus* सफ़ेद बुज्जा

± 72 CM, FRESHWATER MARSH, PONDS AND PADDY FIELDS

**LCR** NT

Also known as the White ibis, it is one of the common resident birds of our wetlands. It is a large white bird with a long, curved black beak and black legs. The bird inhabits wet areas covered with bushes and trees. It is found in small parties, which associate freely with other species of ibises and storks. This bird feeds on various fish, frogs and other water creatures as well as insects. When sated, it rests in little groups standing on the sandbanks, or shallow water, or perched on favoured groups of trees.

# Red-naped Ibis

## *Pseudibis papillosa* काला बुज्जा

± 68 CM, FRESHWATER MARSHES, FALLOW FIELDS AND OPEN COUNTRY

LCR | LC

The Red-naped ibis, also known as the Black ibis, is a large black bird easily identified by its bare red head, nape and long curved beak. Generally found in open country or in cultivated lands, it feeds on the ground, in pairs or in small groups. It is not as dependent on water as other ibises, and is often found in dry fields a good distance away from water. It perches on trees and feeds on the ground. The Red-naped ibis is omnivorous. During droughts, they are known to feed on carrion and insect larvae, and also on decaying meat.

# Eurasian Spoonbill

± 90 CM, FRESHWATER MARSHES AND SHALLOW LAKES

NCR | LC

*Platalea leucorodia* चमचा

A large, white, long-legged wader with a broad, long and flattened bill, expanding into a flat spoon at the tip, the Eurasian spoonbill is widely distributed in wetlands. It is usually found in flocks, which rest by day on the bare margins of the larger, more open jheels or slow-moving rivers. It feeds by day in the company of other waterbirds. The food largely consists of vegetable matter, but all kinds of aquatic insects and their larvae, frogs, molluscs and small fish are also eaten. While feeding, the bird wades quickly through the water with its neck stretched out and the beak half-immersed, turning from side to side with a regular sweeping action, like a man scything grass, so that the beak passes sideways open through the water to close on anything palatable. It is occasionally spotted alongside dormant stretches of river Gomti, some 20 kilometres upstream from the main city, with a bunch of other similar waders.

© Amit Mishra

# CICONIIDAE (Storks)

Storks are large birds and the prominent features of this family are their size, long legs, neck and the bill. They spend most of their lives in wetlands or marshy areas, where they hunt using tactile techniques to capture smaller vertebrates, such as fish, amphibians, reptiles and rodents as well as snails and carrion. The Asian openbill feeds on snails, while adjutants eat a great deal of carrion. Storks are monogamous and show biparental care. Some species are highly colonial nesters. Most aggregations, however, are smaller and sometimes include other species. The large, bulky nests of sticks are typically built in trees.

# Asian Openbill

*Anastomus oscitans* जांघिल

± 68 CM, FRESHWATER SHALLOW LAKES, PONDS, EVEN PUDDLES AND PADDY FIELDS

LCR LC

One of the commonest and most widely distributed storks in India is the Asian openbill. It is found in all well-watered areas in the vicinity of rivers, lakes and marshes. Named after one peculiar physical feature, that is, its long and stout bill with both mandibles slightly curved so as to meet along the base and at the tip, leaving a wide gap just beyond the centre, which is visible even in flight at a distance. The chief food of the openbill is undoubtedly freshwater molluscs, though it occasionally eats fish, crabs and similar organisms. It has been suggested, therefore, that the gap in the beak seems to be an adaptation to easily consume the molluscs.

# Painted Stork

*Mycteria leucocephala* घोंघिल

± 95 CM, FRESHWATER MARSHES, SHALLOW LAKES, PONDS AND EVEN PUDDLES

LCR NT

A common, large bird of well-watered areas all around and commonly spotted in the vicinity of rivers, lakes or even puddles. It has a noticeable long, yellow bill that curves down at the tip, resembling an ibis. The adults have a yellow-orange mask and pinkish legs. It stalks about the shallows with its bill in the water partially open and ready to seize any fish, eel, frog or crab that comes its way. During the heat of the day, it stands motionless in water digesting the morning meal.

They generally nest on thorny trees growing on islands in the lakes. It nests in colonies, hundreds of nests being found together on trees, so closely packed that half a dozen trees may suffice for the whole colony. Some colonies are in remote swamps on the large trees that rise among the water-logged grass and scrub. Tamarind, peepul and banyan trees are usually preferred and the nests are built on the top of the upper boughs, often 60 or 70 feet from the ground, so that the birds can arrive or leave without brushing their wings.

# Woolly-necked Stork

## *Ciconia episcopus* हाजी लगलग

Another large stork of well-watered open country, the Woolly-necked stork frequents flooded or irrigated land, small patches of marshes and rice fields. It is very quiet and sedentary in its habits and, for the most part, stands about in meditation on the ground or feeds in the company of other storks and ibises. Also a good flier, they can be seen soaring like storks and vultures at a great height from the ground. It takes a mixed diet of reptiles, frogs, fish and a variety of other living creatures that it finds in the vicinity of water.

± 90 CM, FLOODED GRASSLANDS, MARSHES, IRRIGATED FIELDS AND RIVERINE AREAS

LCR | NT

# Lesser Adjutant

## *Leptoptilos javanicus* चंदियारी

The Lesser adjutant is a large stork with a completely bare head and neck, ideal for its scavenging habits. In fact, it is a stork which has acquired the habits of vultures. Usually a silent bird, it can produce various calls and noises at breeding sites. It forages by walking and probing into the mud and feeds mainly on aquatic prey, such as fish, amphibians, reptiles and crustaceans. It also consumes locusts, rodents and carrion. At present, the bird has not been reported in Lucknow, but their presence had been noted a few years ago, as per historical accounts.

± 110 CM, MARSHES, FOREST POOLS, LAKES AND DRYING RIVERBEDS

LCR | VU

# PITTIDAE (Pitta)

Because of their brilliant plumage, pittas are sometimes called Jewel Thrushes. All species are stub-tailed, long-legged, and short-necked with a rather stout bill. Only one species of this family has been reported in Lucknow. The Indian pitta is typically colourful, with blue wing plumage. The shimmering colours and bold patterns of these birds often help conceal them from predators against the dappled shade of the forest floor. Pittas are shy birds of forests and scrublands, where they move rapidly, hopping and foraging for insects and snails in the ground litter. All are of great beauty, and the distribution of the various members of the family is very sporadic and curious.

# Indian Pitta

*Pitta brachyura* देसी नौरंग

± 19 CM, BROADLEAVED FOREST WITH DENSE UNDERGROWTH AND ORCHARDS

LCS NT

A unique and lovely bird, the Indian pitta is commonly found in Lucknow. It prefers broadleaved deciduous forests or scrub jungles, and may also be found in gardens and comparatively open country. It has a compact, stout body with a short, stumpy tail, broad, rounded wings and long, stout legs, and, as this structure suggests, it is essentially ground-dwelling bird, hopping and running with great agility. Only a small portion of its time is spent either on the wing or on trees. It is not shy and may easily be approached. The food consists largely of beetles, ants and other insects.

# CHLOROPSEIDAE (Leafbirds)

± 19 CM, BROADLEAVED FORESTS AND SECONDARY GROWTH

NCR | LC

Leafbirds are medium-sized birds with green and yellow plumage and slender, downcurved bill. The only species seen in Lucknow is the Golden-fronted leafbird. Most of the species of leafbirds are usually seen in pairs or in loose flocks. Leafbirds are excellent mimics, and often have an impressive repertoire of sounds that may cause confusion even amongst seasoned birdwatchers.

## Golden-fronted Leafbird

*Chloropsis aurifrons* स्वर्णभाल हरेवा

The Golden-fronted leafbird is brightly coloured—vibrant green, orange-yellow, black, blue and turquoise. The bill of this leafbird is slender with an upper mandible that has a slight downward curve, and encloses the spiked tongue that enables them to easily feed on nectar. It has short sturdy legs and has a habit of dwelling in the top or mid-canopy. It is found in different habitats, ranging from forests to dry scrubs. It is primarily a tree-dweller and seldom touches the ground. Its food consists of nectar, insects, spiders and fruits, such as guava, berries and figs.

© KS Sajwan

# LANIIDAE (Shrikes)

Shrikes are small- to medium-sized birds which have a hooked beak that enables them to catch small animals and insects. They sit upright on the tops of shrubs and other conspicuous perches to spot their prey, and also to advertise their presence to competitors. They prefer living in relatively open spaces. They have raptor-like habits, but they make up for the lack of a raptor's talons by skewering their kills on thorns, or barbed wire, or wedging them into tight places for easy eating. This explains the reason behind their name, which comes from the Latin word for butcher. Most of the shrikes prey on insects, but some larger shrikes also hunt small birds, reptiles and mammals.

- Long-tailed Shrike
- Bay-backed Shrike
- Grey-backed Shrike
- Rufous-tailed or Isabelline Shrike
- Brown Shrike
- Southern or Great Grey Shrike

# Long-tailed Shrike

## *Lanius schach* लम्ब पूँछ लहटोरा

The Long-tailed shrike is a large, noisy shrike, commonly found in open habitats across Asia. The adult bird has a light grey back with variable amount of orange on its lower back and on flanks, and a dark mask, although eastern subspecies have a completely black cap. The Larger Bay-backed shrike has a thicker black mask while the Grey-backed shrike has a dark grey back but lacks the orange and white wings. The juvenile Long-tailed shrike cannot be easily distinguished from other juvenile shrikes.

± 25 CM, BUSHES IN CULTIVATION, OPEN FOREST AND GARDENS

CR | LC

# Southern Grey or Great Grey Shrike

## *Lanius meridionalis* दक्षिणी स्लेटी लहटोरा

A bird of open country, the Southern Grey shrike prefers the more barren stretches of semi-desert country or wide open plains to cultivated lands, and avoids forest areas. It is a solitary bird, but sometimes can be seen in pairs. It captures most of its food on the ground, leaving its vantage point from time to time to fly down after a toothsome morsel. While returning to the perch, it flies low over the ground, and then turns sharply up to settle. Its flight style is undulating but strong. Its food consists largely of beetles, crickets, lizards and ants, and like other shrikes, this species has the habit of impaling surplus food on thorns to form a larder to be eaten later.

© Dr Vivek Banerjee

± 24 CM, OPEN THORN SCRUBS AND CULTIVATION EDGES

LCR | LC

- House Crow
- Indian Jungle Crow
- Rufous Treepie

# CORVIDAE (Crows and Treepies)

Most of the birds that constitute this family are nearly alike in their plumage and habits. Corvids occur in numerous terrestrial habitats. They are found everywhere, from tropical wet forest to deserts, and from the arctic zone to high mountains. They are able to live in harsh conditions, both in extremely cold and hot weather. They are omnivorous and have high cerebral capacity, helping them to take advantage of numerous opportunities for feeding. They vary from medium to large sizes with strong feet, stout bills and large wingspans. Generally territorial, they do not migrate a lot. The male and female birds in this bird family usually look alike.

# House Crow

*Corvus splendens* घरेलू कौआ

The House crow is one of the commonest Indian birds. With its glossy black and grey plumage, it is too familiar a bird to need any description. It is a general scavenger. The House crow feeds largely on the refuse around human habitations, small reptiles and mammals. It is highly gregarious, especially when roosting. Owing to its daring behaviour and activity, the House crow has gained much criticism. But one living thing that habitually gets the better of the House crow—a claim which man certainly cannot make—is the koel. This bird deceives the House crow by substituting its own eggs for those of the crow, and making the latter bring up its young.

± 40 CM, AROUND HUMAN HABITATIONS AND CULTIVATION

CR | LC

# Indian Jungle Crow

*Corvus (macrorhynchos) culminates* जंगली कौआ

As its name implies, in contrast to the House crow, the Indian Jungle crow is a bird of the forests and jungles. It is also an abundant species in the countryside. It is a highly gregarious species and feeds in the company of other birds. Large numbers collect to roost in special patches of forest, though never as many as in the case of the House crow. Like other crows, the Indian Jungle crow is also omnivorous and feeds on scraps of human food, refuse, flying insects, fruit, berries, small mammals and birds, and carrion. It is particularly destructive towards the eggs and young of all birds.

± 41 CM, COUNTRYSIDE AND AROUND CULTIVATION

LCR | LC

# Rufous Treepie

± 48 CM, GARDENS, WOODED OPEN COUNTRY AND AROUND HUMAN HABITATIONS

CR | LC

*Dendrocitta vegabunda* लाल तरुपिक

The treepie is, as its name denotes, essentially arboreal, and rarely known to visit the ground. It is widely distributed and a common bird of gardens and open forests. A fairly shy bird, it lives amidst thick foliage, and usually offers only glimpses of itself as it flies from tree to tree. Mainly arboreal, it sometimes descends lower into bushes and onto the ground to pick up termites. A bold predator and a noisy bird, it is more heard than seen. The food consists of fruit, berries, insects, caterpillars, lizards and small snakes.

# ORIOLIDAE (Orioles)

Orioles are bright, golden-yellow perching birds and common in the city. They are boldly patterned, especially the males, with black and golden-yellow in the plumage. Orioles are very active creatures, full of the joy of life, and they delight to indulge in aerial games, following each other from tree to tree, darting through the foliage with their bright plumage flashing in the sun. They have a range of melodious notes, freely uttered on such occasions. All the species are insectivorous, but occasionally, feed on fruits as well. They are found in areas covered with old, leafy trees.

- Indian Golden Oriole
- Black-hooded Oriole

# Indian Golden Oriole

± 25 CM, FOREST, ORCHARDS AND GARDENS AROUND HUMAN HABITATIONS

CW | LC

*Oriolus (oriolus) kundoo* स्वर्ण पीलक

The male Golden oriole has a striking black and yellow plumage, while the female is a drabber green bird. It is strictly arboreal, never descending, as a rule, neither to the undergrowth nor to the ground. It is very shy and secretive, keeping to the thickest portions of the boughs. It is known by its voice and not its appearance. It feeds on insects and fruits. It has a pleasant call, often heard in gardens and forests. It is fairly common in Lucknow.

# Black-hooded Oriole

± 25 CM, OPEN, WELL-WOODED AND BROADLEAVED FORESTS

CW | LC

*Oriolus xanthornus* टोपीदार पीलक

The Black-hooded oriole is a bright golden bird with black head, wings and tail. This very active and noisy bird is found in fairly well-timbered country and is especially partial to groves, avenues and gardens. It is an arboreal species, though occasionally, it descends to the ground to capture insects. Its main food, however, remains the fruits of the various species of wild figs. It is found singly or in pairs, though the family parties keep together for a short time after the young ones are fledged.

# CAMPEPHAGIDAE (Minivets and Cuckooshrikes)

Minivets are one of the most beautiful birds with striking colours, mostly vibrant shades of red and yellow. Principally, minivets belong to hilly areas and descend to distant plains in deep winter. They are agile and strictly arboreal. These little colourful birds, flitting among the foliage of trees in flocks, are a pleasant sight to behold.

- Small Minivet
- Long-tailed Minivet
- Scarlet Minivet
- Large Cuckooshrike
- Common Woodshrike
- Black-winged Cuckooshrike
- Black-headed Cuckooshrike
- Bar-winged Flycatcher Shrike

# Long-tailed Minivet

*Pericrocotus ethologus* छोटा पहाड़ी राजालाल

± 20 CM, FORESTS AND WELL-WOODED AREAS (WINTER)

LCW LC

The Long-tailed minivet is one of the many species found in the northern part of our country. Slightly larger than the House sparrow, this is one of the most striking bird species. Both the male and the female birds have different colour composition. The male has attractive orange-red underparts, while the female has an indistinct yellow wash on the forehead and supercilium. An arboreal bird, it rarely descends to the ground. It feeds on insects by flitting about in the foliage to glean its prey from leaves, buds and bark. This bird can be spotted in small groups, in Lucknow, during the winter season.

# Common Woodshrike

± 18 CM, OPEN BROADLEAVED FOREST AND SECONDARY GROWTH

**NCR** LC

*Tephrodornis pondicerianus* सामान्य तरती टुइयां

A medium-sized, ashy-brown bird, it has a noticeable hooked bill and fairly large head. It is mainly arboreal and forages usually on the trees by gleaning insects from the foliage, branches and trunk of the trees. Though they occasionally forage on the ground as well. In Lucknow, old palatial premises with green cover, countryside with light forest and scrub habitats are where the bird can be spotted in the company of other insectivorous birds.

# RHIPIDURIDAE (Fantails)

**Fantails are sparrow-sized birds and fidgety in nature. They have a habit of constantly wagging and spreading their distinctive rounded tail like a fan. When the tail is folded, it is rounded at the end, but when spread out for display or aerial foraging, it has a characteristic fan-like shape that gives the family its name. Mostly arboreal, keeping to the lower and middle storeys, but often descending to the lower vegetation, and seldom to the ground. Overall, fantails are strong fliers, supported by tapered wings.**

- White-throated Fantail
- White-browed Fantail

# White-throated Fantail

## *Rhipidura albicolis* चकदिल नचनी

The White-throated fantail is slightly bigger than the sparrow. It has a dark fan-shaped tail with white edges. It is found in a variety of forest habitats where it feeds on insects caught either in the air or on the ground. It often fans its tail as it moves through the undergrowth. It is found throughout the Indian subcontinent and southeast Asia, in the foothills and adjacent plains, up to a height of 13,000 metres.

± 18 CM, FORESTS, WOODED AREAS AND SECONDARY GROWTH

CW | LC

# DICRURIDAE (Drongos)

Drongos are mostly black or dark grey, short-legged birds, with an upright stance when perched. They have forked tails and some have elaborate tail decorations. They feed on insects which they catch in flight or on the ground. Some species are accomplished mimics and have a variety of alarm calls, to which other birds and animals often respond. There is evidence that they utter hoax alarm calls that typically scare other animals off food, which the drongo then eats. These insectivorous birds are usually found in open forests or bush. One of the species, the Greater Racket-tailed drongo, is noted for its ability to mimic other birds and even mammals. Drongos are also known as aggressive and fearless birds, and will attack much larger species if their nest or young are threatened.

- Black Drongo
- Spangled or Hair-crested Drongo
- Ashy Drongo
- Greater Racket-tailed Drongo
- Lesser Racket-tailed Drongo
- White-bellied Drongo

# Black Drongo

*Dicrurus macrocercus* सामान्य भुजंगा

± 28 CM, AROUND HUMAN HABITATIONS AND CULTIVATION

CR | LC

The Black drongo, also known as the King crow, is an all-black, medium-sized bird with a long forked tail and a strong bill. It is known for its aggressive behaviour towards much larger birds, such as crows, and never hesitates to dive-bomb any bird of prey that invades its territory. This insectivorous bird is usually solitary or moves about in pairs. Small birds nest near the drongo's nest to feel protected. It is common in open countryside habitats, such as farms, fields and wetlands, where it perches on a vantage point, and pounces on or chases unsuspecting insects, small birds and small invertebrates.

# Ashy Drongo

## *Dicrurus leucophaeus* स्लेटी भुजंगा

The Ashy drongo has a dark grey and slate grey plumage, and a long, slim, forked tail. It has short legs and sits upright on a perch, often high on a tree. It is quite common in wooded habitats, where it sallies for insects and aggressively chases other birds that may compete for food or nectar. Most birds migrate southwards every winter. Similar to the Black drongo, but slimmer, it is found in different habitats. Its call includes both harsh and sweet notes, and it can mimic some bird species, albeit poorly.

± 18 CM, WELL-WOODED AREAS

NCW | LC

# White-bellied Drongo

## *Dicrurus caerulescens* सफ़ेद पेट भुजंगा

As the name suggests, this bird has a white belly and a blackish-blue plumage. It prefers light forests, bamboos, and generally avoids cultivated lands and treeless open country. Often seen singly or in groups of up to three birds, it sometimes joins mixed-species foraging flocks. They perch upright close to the top of trees and capture insects in the air with short aerobatic sallies. Mostly insectivorous, it feeds on winged insects, such as crickets, grasshoppers, moths and winged termites called alates (patinga of Urdu shairi).

± 24 CM, OPEN FORESTS AND WELL-WOODED AREAS

NCR | LC

# Greater Racket-tailed Drongo

± 32 CM, BROADLEAVED FORESTS AND WELL-WOODED AREAS

NCR | LC

*Dicrurus paradiseus* बड़ा भीमराज भुजंगा

It is a glossy blackbird, immediately identified by its plumed crest and the extraordinary development of the outer tail-feathers into rackets at the end. Popularly known as the Bhimraj, it is a forest species and prefers the densest and dampest of the Indian forests, though it is also found in any well-wooded country, and even in gardens. It is often seen in parties of four or five, which appear to wander a good deal in search of food, flying from tree to tree, swooping at insects on the wing or capturing them from the branches. Its food consists of a variety of insects, wasps, beetles, butterflies, locusts and their larvae. It is also known to feed on bees.

# MONARCHIDAE (Monarchs and Paradise Flycatchers)

Birds in this family are small, insectivorous songbirds with long tails and broad bills. Their plumage ranges from sombre to spectacular. They inhabit forests and only a few species migrate with the change in season. Many species decorate their cup-shaped nests with lichen. In Lucknow, there is seasonally, that is, during summer, always a chance to have a glimpse of these flying beauties in heritage buildings with well-wooded areas.

- Black-naped Monarch
- Asian Paradise Flycatcher

# Black-naped Monarch

*Hypothymis azurea* काला कटकटिया

± 16 CM, BROADLEAVED FORESTS, GARDENS AND WELL-WOODED COMPOUNDS

NCW | LC

Black-naped monarch is a beautiful bird. The azure-blue male bird exhibits a black nape patch and a thin black gorget, while the female lacks the black nape patch and gorget markings. It has short legs and sits upright whilst perched prominently, like a shrike. Primarily an insectivorous, the bird can often be seen hunting insects. When alarmed or alert, the nape feathers are raised into a pointed crest without markings.

© Rajesh Panwar

# Asian Paradise Flycatcher

± 20 CM, FORESTS AND WELL-WOODED AREAS

**LCS** LC

*Terpsiphone paradisi* दूधराज

This graceful flycatcher has been aptly named. The long wavy tail plumes are reminiscent of the ornaments of the true birds of paradise. The sheer beauty, and grace of form and movement, make the adult male bird's beauty unrivalled in India. Males occur in two morphs, one with a rufous or glossy chestnut upper plumage and another with a white or dirty white plumage. This species is purely arboreal, its feet being too short and weak for progress on the ground. All food is acquired on the wing, and that the bird is capable of speed and skill in the air is proven by the fact that it manages to catch dragonflies as well. It has been spotted nearly all over the country, and appears in Lucknow during the summer months.

© Amit Mishra

# AEGITHINIDAE (Ioras)

Birds in this family are small, insectivorous songbirds with broad bills. Their plumage ranges from sombre to spectacular. They inhabit forests and only a few species migrate with the change in season. Many species decorate their cup-shaped nests with lichen. In Lucknow, during summer, there is always a chance to catch a glimpse of these flying beauties in heritage buildings with well-wooded areas.

- Common Iora
- Marshall Iora

# Common Iora

## *Aegithina tiphia* सामान्य शोबीगी

± 14 CM, EDGES OF FOREST, CULTIVATION, GARDENS IN AND AROUND HUMAN HABITATIONS

CR | LC

The Common iora is a little, greenish-yellow, sparrow-sized bird. It is a familiar garden bird in the greater part of India, frequenting the outskirts of villages and cultivated lands as well as the edges of forests and scrub jungles. It is usually found in pairs, although occasionally, two or three birds might be seen on the same tree, looking for insects. It can produce a variety of notes and some mournful whistles. It feeds mainly on insects, searching for them from their perches high in the canopy. It may sometimes hang upside down from branches. It catches insects on the wing. It is a fairly common bird in the city.

Common Iora (Male)

Common Iora (Female)

# TURDIDAE (Thrushes)

The birds known as Thrush, come in a variety of colours and patterns including brown, blue, grey and black. They often have patches of red, orange, white or yellow. They are plump, soft-plumaged and small- to medium-sized birds, inhabiting wooded areas. They often feed on the ground or eat small fruit. They are insectivorous, but most species also eat worms, snails and fruits. Some species are considered to be among the most beautiful in the avian world.

- Blue-capped Rock Thrush
- Blue Rock Thrush
- Orange-headed Thrush
- Scaly Thrush
- Tickell's Thrush
- Grey-winged Blackbird
- Dark or Black-throated Thrush

# Blue Rock Thrush

± 20 CM, ALONGSIDE STREAMS AND ROCKY AREAS

NCW LC

*Monticola solitarius* कश्मीरी शैल कस्तूरा

The Blue Rock thrush is a dark-coloured bird—the male bluish and the female speckled with buff and brown. In the breeding season in the hills, it is very much a bird of the rocks, frequenting boulder-clad hillsides and open rocky ground. When breeding at a lower height, it can be seen in the tree zone, rocky screes, gorges or cliffs in the open ground between the forests. In the absence of rocks, the bird finds a substitute in quarries, ruined forts and unoccupied buildings. Perched on a point of vantage—be it a boulder or cornice—it sits very erect and alone. It is omnivorous and feeds on insects, larvae, worms, snails, lizards, berries and seeds.

# Orange-headed Thrush

*Zoothera citrina* केसरी सर कस्तूरा

± 20 CM, SHADY FOREST AND WELL-WOODED AREAS

NCR | LC

A medium-sized ground thrush with orange and grey plumage, the Orange-headed thrush is essentially a forest-loving species and mostly found in damp and shady thickets, or in thick bamboo-brakes, where it feeds alone on the ground under thick tangles of roots and stems. It is a shy and quiet bird, and when disturbed, promptly flies up to a bough, where it sits silent and motionless waiting to resume its quest for food. Most active at dawn and dusk, it probes the leaf litter for insects and their larvae, spiders, other invertebrates and fruit.

# Tickell's Thrush

± 21 CM, GROVES AND WELL-WOODED AREAS

NCW LC

*Turdus unicolor* देसी पवई कस्तूरा

The Tickell's thrush is common in the open forest in the Himalayas and migrates seasonally into peninsular India. It is named after the British ornithologist, Samuel Tickell. It is an omnivorous bird, feeding on a wide range of insects, earthworms and berries. It nests in bushes or similar places. Though not seen in flocks, it forms loose groups of two to five members. In Lucknow, sporadic sightings of the bird have been reported at the Sanjay Gandhi Post Graduate Institute campus. There is one fascinating aspect of its feeding behaviour that needs to be mentioned here. When looking for food, it often stops with its head cocked to one side to listen for the insect larva and earthworms. It is an uncommon winter visitor in Lucknow.

© KS Sajwan

# MUSCICAPIDAE (Flycatchers, Chats and Redstarts)

It is one of the largest bird families. Birds in this category vary from small to medium in size, and are known to be arboreal insectivores. Characterised by an upright stance when perched, they possess varied appearances, weak songs and harsh calls. Flycatchers are found in almost every environment with an ideal nature scape. Most of the flycatcher species migrate to the south in winter.

Chats belong to a diverse range of birds inhabiting a variety of habitats. A few species among them are common in urban environs and seen almost round the year. Though arboreal, most of the birds in the family do spend a considerable amount of time on the ground. They are insectivorous.

Redstarts are primarily insectivorous. They mostly feed on the ground. Most of the redstarts have a red tail.

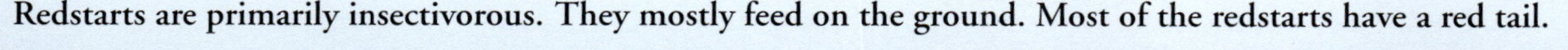

- Rufous-gorgeted Flycatcher
- Red-throated or Red-breasted Flycatcher
- Asian Brown Flycatcher
- Taiga Flycatcher
- Tickell's Blue Flycatcher
- Little Pied Flycatcher
- Ultramarine Flycatcher
- Blue-throated Flycatcher
- Verditer Flycatcher
- Grey-headed Canary Flycatcher
- Siberian Rubythroat
- White-tailed or Himalayan Rubythroat
- Bluethroat
- Oriental Magpie Robin
- Indian Robin
- Black Redstart
- Common or Siberian Stonechat
- Pied Bushchat
- Grey Bushchat
- Brown Rockchat

# Rufous-gorgeted Flycatcher

± 14 CM, DENSE OR OPEN FORESTS, FOREST CLEARINGS AND GARDENS

NCW LC

*Ficedula strophiata* लालकंठ मछरिया

A fairly lesser-known flycatcher species from the Himalayas, this bird has a rufous gorget and white coloration on the sides of its black tail. Known as a short-distance and altitudinal migrant, it migrates to lower altitudes after breeding during the winter. It is found in forests and thick scrubs. This solitary bird is sometimes seen in pairs as well. Its diet is mostly small invertebrates. It forages on the ground or in the undergrowth. It is an occasional visitor to Lucknow.

© KS Sajwan

# Ultramarine Flycatcher

*Ficedula superciliaris* समुद्रीनील मछरिया

A small arboreal flycatcher, it breeds in the foothills of the Himalayas, and is seen in southern India in winters. Usually alone, it sometimes joins mixed hunting parties. It mostly keeps to the low trees and bushes, feeding among the foliage canopy, not venturing much into the open. This flycatcher constantly jerks up its tail, often accompanied by a fluffing of the head feathers and a 'trrr' note, especially in proximity of nest. It hunts in the characteristic style of flycatchers, rarely venturing out in the open. Its diet mainly consists of insects. Lucknow functions as a stop over during migration for the bird.

± 12 CM, OPEN DECIDUOUS FORESTS, GARDENS AND ORCHARDS

PM | LC

# Verditer Flycatcher

*Eumyias thalassinus* वर्डीटर मछरिया

It has a conspicuous verditer-blue colour and is a winter visitor. It is a bold and secretive bird, frequenting jungles and gardens alike, and perching on open, exposed positions, hawking insects in the air with active flight. Its brilliant colouring catches the sunlight and renders it conspicuous.

During the winter months, it appears in country habitats that have large trees. Its usual perch is a bare twig at the top of a tree, but it is also partial to telegraph wires.

± 16 CM, OPEN FOREST, GARDENS

LCW | LC

# Grey-headed Canary Flycatcher

± 13 CM, FORESTS AND WOODED AREAS

LCW LC

*Culicicapa ceylonensis* पिलपेटी मछरिया

Small, greenish-yellow, with an ashy head and neck, the Grey-headed Canary flycatcher is a bird of well-wooded areas, where trees provide wide shady arcades chequered with occasional patches of sunlight. It can be seen hawking insects in the air as it flits incessantly from bough to bough, sometimes catching the gleams of sunlight, and sometimes, hidden in the gloom, eternally restless, eternally cheerful.

# Red-breasted Flycatcher

## *Ficedula parva* सीफिया मछरिया

± 12 CM, OPEN FORESTS, SCRUB AT CULTIVATION EDGES AND GARDENS

**LCW** LC

The Red-breasted flycatcher is a distinctive, small, brown bird. The male bird has a rusty-orange throat and the colour continues onto the breast. This bird prefers well-wooded areas provided that there is sufficient tree cover, it does not matter whether it is a forest, cultivated land or a neighbourhood of towns and villages. It is known to frequent shady places within the boughs of large trees in which it sedately hawks and flits from bough to bough. When perched, its tail is often held cocked with wingtips drooping.

In Lucknow, this bird is seen in winter, and sometimes, it stays till early summer.

Red-breasted Flycatcher (Female)

Red-breasted Flycatcher (Male)

© Rajesh Panwar

# Bluethroat

± 15 CM, TALL GRASS, SCRUBS AND GARDENS

CW LC

*Luscinia svecica* नीलकंठी लुसिनिया

The bird has earned its name due to its spectacular blue bib circled by a rufous crescent. It is a bird of the ground and prefers damp spots, such as reed beds on the edge of jheels, tamarisk thickets in riverbeds, heavy standing crops and similar locations with enough cover. It feeds on the ground, turning over the leaves and soil to expose small invertebrates. Occasionally, it ascends to the top of the bushes to look around. A common winter visitor to Lucknow, it is found in scrubby waterside and reedbeds.

© Ashish Loya

# White-tailed or Himalayan Rubythroat

## *Luscinia pectoralis* श्वेतपुच्छी माणिक कंठी

Primarily from the Himalayas, the Himalayan rubythroat moves to lower elevations and returns to higher altitudes in summer. In winter, its natural habitats include open woodlands and scrubs. It is usually seen singly or in pairs, during the breeding season. The bird feeds mainly on small insects, including beetles and ants. The parents forage close to the nest and the young are mainly fed with hairy caterpillars. The Himalayan rubythroat is not commonly found in the region.

± 14 CM, MARSHES WITH EDGED GRASS COVER

PM | LC

# Siberian Rubythroat

## *Luscinia calliope* साईबेरियाई माणिक कंठी

One of the numerous small birds that visit Lucknow in winter, the Siberian rubythroat prefers to inhabit areas of open grasslands, scrubs and thickets. The bird is fairly terrestrial and forages on the ground, in bushes and also around cultivated fields, parks and gardens. It feeds primarily on insects and larvae, besides ants, wasp, beetles, bugs and spiders.

© KS Sajwan

± 14 CM, BUSHES AND THICK UNDERGROWTH

PM | LC

## Oriental Magpie Robin

*Copsychus saularis* दयाल

Dayal, as the Oriental Magpie robin is most lovingly called in this part, is claimed to be one of the most familiar birds found about the haunts of man. An equally familiar garden bird, it delights in the mixed chequer of sunshine and shade that is characteristic of an Indian garden. It is fascinating to observe the male bird early in the morning, and again in the evening, as it perches on the topmost bough of one of the garden trees and pours out its beautiful song. It is one of the best songbirds in a land where singing birds are somewhat scarce. It obtains its food from the ground, which consists of insects, grasshoppers, crickets, ants and beetles. It also feeds on a little vegetable matter, and occasionally, on earthworms.

± 20 CM, OPEN BROADLEAVED FORESTS, GROVES AND GARDENS

## Indian Robin

*Saxicoloides fulicatus* कलचुरी

A nondescript bird, the Indian robin is primarily black with chestnut bottom feathers. This robin is generally seen in pairs, foraging on the ground with the tail cocked up. It is a familiar bird, hanging around the haunts of men, the outskirts of villages, buildings both great and small, brick-kilns and similar locations. In addition, it is also partial to stony, barren hillsides and dry ravines. In fact, the essential conditions for its presence are dry, open countryside. The Sanjay Gandhi Post Graduate Institute and the National Botanical Research Institute host this bird in their campus.

± 19 CM, WELL-WOODED AREAS, SCRUBS AND CULTIVATION EDGES

CR | LC

# Black Redstart

## *Phoenicurus ochruros* काला थिरथिरा

± 15 CM, CULTIVATION, GARDENS AND PLANTATIONS

CW | LC

The Black redstart is one of the most pleasant and friendly of our garden visitors during the winter months. It is a local migratory species and occupies varied open habitats. It feeds mainly on or near the ground. The bird is easy to observe as it perches rather upright on poles, rocks and stumps, and sings from prominent perches. One can observe the characteristic shivering of the tail and jerky body movements of the bird as it makes short dashes to the ground, soon returning to perch with a catch. It is often spotted within the premises of Raj Bhavan, the Sanjay Gandhi Post Graduate Institute and other sites with lavish vegetation.

# Common or Siberian Stonechat

± 12 CM, SCRUBLANDS, REED BEDS AND CULTIVATION

CW | LC

*Saxicola torquatus* सामान्य भट्ट पिद्दा

The Common stonechat is another small bird of open cultivation, particularly partial to fields with standing crops of cotton, sugarcane or cereals. It invariably perches on some vantage point—either a large stone, or more generally, the topmost twig of a bush or plant—and thence makes short flights in all directions to capture some insect on the ground, either devouring it on the spot or taking it back to its perch. It is a winter visitor.

# Pied Bushchat

## *Saxicola caprata* अबलक झाड़ी पिद्दा

The Pied bushchat is one of the most familiar birds in India. The male bird is small, with conspicuous little black and white colour, while the female is dark brown. It is commonly found in the plains, and also hills. It avoids heavy forests but is common about cultivated lands, grasslands and scrub jungles. This solitary bird takes up a position on the top of a stake, tuft of grass or some other exposed perch from where it makes frequent little darts to the ground to pick up an unwary grasshopper or bug. It is quite common in Lucknow.

± 12 CM, OPEN COUNTRY, CULTIVATION AND TALL GRASS

# Brown Rockchat

## *Cercomela fusca* थरथरीकंपनी

The Brown rockchat is a common and familiar species found in arid stony wastes, earthy cliffs, on rocky hills, and in and about villages and towns. It is known to frequent buildings, flit in and out of empty chambers and gaping windows of ancient palaces and forts, and perches on the cornices of tombs and mosques. Its food consists of insects, beetles, ants and the like, which it captures on the ground, flying down from the elevated spots where it perches. In Lucknow, the bird can be easily spotted at old heritage structures.

± 17 CM, URBAN GARDENS, OLD BUILDINGS AND CLIFFS

# SITTIDAE (Nuthatches, Wallcreepers)

Nuthatches are characterised by large heads, short tails and powerful bills and feet. They advertise their territory using loud and simple songs. They are omnivorous and eat mostly insects, nuts and seeds. They forage for insects hidden in or under a tree bark by climbing along tree trunks and branches, sometimes upside down. Nuthatches are highly vocal and produce an assortment of whistles, trills and calls.

## Indian Nuthatch

*Sitta castanea* खैरापेट सिरी

The Indian nuthatch is a small bird with slaty-blue back and chestnut-bay underparts. It is a fairly common bird in Lucknow. Purely arboreal, it runs like a mouse about the bark and twigs of trees, frequently upside down. It shares the ability of woodpeckers and treecreepers to climb about the trunks and branches of trees in order to search the crevices of the bark for insects and larvae, hidden from the sight of most insect-feeding birds. Mostly seen in pairs or in small groups, they often move about in the company of other species as well.

± 12 CM, BROADLEAVED FOREST, GARDENS AND GROVES

**CR** | LC

# STURNIDAE (Mynahs and Starlings)

Birds in this group are 6 to 14 inches in size with a long, cone-shaped bill. Most of the birds in this family gather in noisy flocks, large to very large in size. They forage on the ground and eat insects and seeds, besides looking for human refuse. Many Asian species, particularly the larger ones, are called mynahs, and many African species are known as glossy starlings because of their iridescent plumage.

- Chestnut-tailed Starling
- Brahminy Starling
- Rosy Starling
- Common or European Starling
- Asian Pied Starling
- Common Mynah
- Bank Mynah
- Jungle Mynah

# Common Mynah

*Acridotheres tristis* देसी मैना

Common mynah is one of the most abundant birds in our country. Like the House crow, this bird is ubiquitous and known to be present within human habitation, be it a populous city or a remote village. It normally lives in pairs or groups and there is a very obvious affection among them. It feeds with the group on the ground. An accomplished scavenger, this bird feeds on almost anything, including insects, fruits and vegetables, scraps, pet food and even fledgeling birds. In the evening, it gathers with other groups for communal roosts, under the roof of bridges and large trees.

± 25 CM, HUMAN HABITATIONS AND CULTIVATION

**CR** | LC

# Bank Mynah

*Acridotheres ginginianus* गंगा मैना

The Bank mynah strongly resembles the Common mynah in demeanour and general effect, but its wattle is red instead of yellow. Its is often found in company of the Common mynah and has very similar habits. Usually observed in small, scattered groups around human habitations, this bold and confident bird is often seen along roadside restaurants picking up scraps. It nests almost exclusively in the earthen banks of rivers, where it digs holes and breeds in large colonies. Its name comes from this preference for riverbanks. It is interesting to see it follow grazing animals, picking up disturbed insects or even ticks on the animals.

± 23 CM, HUMAN HABITATIONS, CULTIVATION AND OPEN COUNTRYSIDE

**LCR** | LC

# Jungle Mynah

*Acridotheres fuscus* जंगली मैना

± 23 CM, CULTIVATION NEAR WELL-WOODED AREAS AND EDGES OF HUMAN HABITATION

LCR | LC

The Jungle mynah is widely spread in the Himalayas and in parts of the Indian plains. It is fairly easy to recognise because of the tuft of feathers on its forehead and orange-yellow bill. As its name indicates, this mynah is a bird of the forest, though it often associates with the Common mynah, and frequents the neighbourhood of houses. When in flight, its habit, gait and behaviour greatly resembles the Common mynah, except that it is neither bold nor a scavenger. But it is often mistaken by most people for the Common mynah. The bird inhabits open forests, cultivated fields and areas around waterbodies. It is often seen around grazing cattle. It is omnivorous and feeds mainly on insects, fruit and seeds.

# Chestnut-tailed Starling

± 20 CM, OPEN WELL-WOODED AREAS AND LARGE GARDENS

**LCR** LC

*Sturnia malabarica* पवई मैना

Also known as the Grey-headed mynah, it is a silver bird with finely hackled head and neck. Purely arboreal, than most other species of mynahs and starlings, it is shy and difficult to observe. It is usually found in parties and small flocks which frequent treetops, and indulge in a good deal of squabbling and chasing about from branch to branch, especially when the attraction is the flowers of the coral-tree or the silk-cotton tree. At times, the flocks descend and feed on the ground. It is an omnivorous bird and feeds on fruit, nectar and insects.

# Brahminy Starling

*Sturnia pogodarum* पुहैय्या

± 21 CM, DRY WELL-WOODED AREAS AND HUMAN HABITATIONS

**LCR** LC

Popularly known as 'Pawi' or 'Papaya', it is a familiar bird and comes a good deal into folklore. It is a rather small, sprightly bird, with the top of the head black and crested. It is partial to open, well-cultivated localities with sumptuous tree cover, and is tame and familiar in its habits, neither avoids nor seeks the neighbourhood of man. It feeds, for the most part, on the ground, often in company of other species of mynahs and starlings, retiring, when sated, to the trees in which it normally lives. It is found singly, in pairs and in small parties as well. It has a wide repertoire of calls and are also given to mimicking other species.

# Rosy Starling

*Pastor roseus* गुलाबी मैना

A handsome crested bird, the Rosy starling is rose-pink with black head, wings and tail. It collects in flocks, which feed on fruits and berries, grubs, insects, grasshoppers and locusts (being particularly useful in the elimination of locusts) in every type of open country. Also known as Rosy pastors, they feed largely on the ground; and when a field of grass is being irrigated, a pink and black cloud of these birds is often seen in pursuit of the flooded-out insect life, quarrelling and chattering and jumping into the air as the flock moves along. Like other starlings, it is highly gregarious, forming large winter flocks.

± 21 CM, DAMP, GRASSY AREAS AND CULTIVATION

**NCR** LC

# Common Starling

## *Sturnus vulgaris* तिल्यर मैना

Also known as the European starling, the Common starling is a bird of cultivated lands in the open plains. It is sometimes seen in the company of mynahs and Rosy starlings. It forms large flocks in winter, and the chief characteristic of these flocks is the haste with which they feed on the ground, digging their bills into the crevices of the soil and extracting various grubs and insects on which they feed. The flock always advances with a bustle and hurry, with the bird not just hopping but taking quick purposeful steps. The birds in the rear frequently fly over to settle in front of the leaders. It feeds on fruits, berries and grains as well.

± 21 CM, CULTIVATION AND DAMP GRASSLANDS

LCR LC

© Amit Mishra

# Asian Pied Starling

*Gracupica contra* अबलकी मैना

± 23 CM, PUBLIC PARKS, HUMAN HABITATIONS AND CULTIVATION

**CR** LC

Also known as the Pied mynah, the Asian Pied mynah is a conspicuously pied black-and-white bird. It differs from the Common mynah in the fact that it is a bird of open cultivation and never enters or perches on houses, though, it may frequently be found in gardens. It is common to a number of habitats, living generally in small parties that spend time hunting in grasslands, where the pied plumage renders them conspicuous. This insectivorous bird catches grasshoppers, crickets and beetles on the ground, and extracts caterpillars, ants, worms and other insects from amongst the roots of grass. It is an all-season bird of Lucknow.

# AEGITHALIDAE (Tits)

Tits are very active and chirpy birds, also known as Bushtits or Long-tailed. This family of small, drab birds is strictly arboreal and insectivorous. But many of the species in the family depend on seeds, particularly from trees, in winter. They probe bark crevices, branches and leaves for insects. Out of the 15 species of tits in the Indian subcontinent, most inhabit the Himalayas and only one species is known to descend from the mountains, seasonally.

## Cinereous Tit

*Parus cinereus* स्लेटी रामगंगरा

Also known as the Great tit, the Cinereous tit is a grey, black and off-white bird of light woodlands. A proper bird of the hills, it prefers open forests. Though arboreal, it also wanders freely into bushes and scrub jungles, frequently visiting the ground in search of food. It feeds in the middle- and upper-strata of forests as well as in gardens and cultivated areas. This bird avoids dense forests. In Lucknow, it is more or less found in gardens and near river or canal banks with bush growth. The huge premises of the National Botanical Research Institute, the Sanjay Gandhi Post Graduate Institute, areas of Cantonment and Janeshwar Mishra Park are a few sites where spotting this bird is a sure bet.

± 14 CM, FORESTS, WELL-WOODED AREAS AND GARDENS

CR LC

# HIRUNDINIDAE (Swallows and Martins)

Swallows and martins are a group of passerines and are characterised by their adaptation to aerial feeding. These birds have characteristically long, slender body and long, pointed wings. Many species have long, forked tails as well. In most species, males and females look alike. Birds of this family depend on insects and catch them on the wing. Most species live and travel in flocks. These flocks are often seen perched on electric wires. Swallows typically build mud nests close to overhead shelters, in locations that are protected from both the weather and predators.

- Barn Swallow
- Wire-tailed Swallow
- Red-rumped Swallow
- Streak-throated Swallow
- Eurasian Crag Martin
- Pale Sand Martin
- Plain Martin or Grey-throated Martin
- Dusky Crag Martin

# Streak-throated Swallow

*Petrochelidon fluvicola* नहर अबाबील

The Streak-throated swallow or the Indian Cliff swallow is a small, dusky swallow with a notched, long, broad tail. It inhabits cultivated open country near water, reservoirs, wilderness close to wetlands, towns and villages.

Their diet consists almost entirely of flies. They hawk in flocks, sometimes with other species of swallows.

± 11 CM, CULTIVATION, OPEN COUNTRY NEAR WATER (CANALS AND RIVERS)

CR | LC

# Red-tumped Swallow

*Cecropis daurica* लालपुट्ठी अबाबील

The Red-rumped, Striated or Mosque swallow is rather large, with a more deeply-forked tail and chestnut rump. Always found in pairs or groups, it spends a greater part of the day on the wing, flying backwards and forwards over a self-appointed beat, hawking at insects on the wing, while occasionally resting on telegraph wires. Like the other members of the family, this swallow is chiefly remarkable for its nesting habits. The nest is a remarkable structure of fine mud pellets collected by the birds, a mouthful at a time, from the edges of puddles. It takes several weeks to build this kind of retort-shaped nests. The Red-rumped swallow always builds its nest under rocks or culverts, or bridges, or the ceilings of houses and verandahs.

± 16 CM, CULTIVATION, OPEN COUNTRY AND FOREST CLEARINGS

LCW | LC

# Wire-tailed Swallow

± 14 CM, CULTIVATION AND OPEN COUNTRY NEAR WATER (CANAL AND RIVERS)

CR | LC

*Hirundo smithii* लीशरा अबाबील

Common in plains and lower hills, the Wire-tailed swallow is essentially a bird found near water. In particular, it is fond of the great canals and likes skimming over their surface with its long tail-wires conspicuous, and its bright colours flashing in the sun. The female bird and the young have shorter tails. Where canals are not available, it frequents the neighbouring areas with rivers, streams and lakes, and it is also partial to rice fields.

© Amit Mishra

# Plain Martin

*Riparia paludicola* सामान्य अबालि

± 12 CM, AROUND RIVERS, STREAMS AND SANDBANKS

LCW | LC

A common bird of the plains, the Plain martin is a small, plain brown swallow with a white belly. Generally this bird, in small- to medium-sized groups, can be seen incessantly flying about sandy banks of water channels. It uses different habitats, usually near water. It nests in sandy cliffs and banks, generally choosing those in the vicinity of running water, though occasionally, it moves to banks over ponds or in dry nullahs. They feed almost invariably in the vicinity of water and spend a greater part of their lives hawking insects, high or low in the air, according to circumstances, over the surface of swiftly-flowing rivers or the placid waters of lakes and tanks. The Plain martin is a winter visitor to Lucknow.

# PYCNONOTIDAE (Bulbuls)

Bulbuls are medium-sized songbirds with short neck and long tail. They go about in pairs or in small groups and constantly emit a cheery note. Highly vocal and resistant to human pressures on the environment, they are tolerant of disturbed habitat. They are more often found in gardens rather than in the open country. They frequent trees and bushes, and are rarely seen on the ground.

Bulbuls build cup-shaped nests, a neatly woven structure among bushy plants in gardens and even in the verandahs of the houses.

Two species, Red-whiskered and Red-vented bulbuls have been, since historical times, captured in great numbers for pet trade, and for this reason, have been widely introduced to tropical and subtropical areas.

- Red-whiskered Bulbul
- Red-vented Bulbul

# Red-whiskered Bulbul

*Pycnonotus jocosus* सिपाही बुलबुल

± 20 CM, OPEN FORESTS, SECONDARY GROWTH AND URBAN HABITATIONS

CR LC

The Red-whiskered bulbul, or the Crested bulbul, is a common bird of Lucknow. Owing to a large white and a small crimson patch on each of the cheeks, the bird was named red-whiskered. It is a cheerful, lively bird and prefers to live in the haunts of humans and are found freely in gardens, bamboo clumps, orchards, cultivated ares, low-scrub jungles and the neighbourhood of villages.

According to historical accounts, termed as a popular cage bird, this species of bulbul is mentioned as a common species, closely intermingled with the human life.

CW Smith says these birds are in great request among the natives, being of a fearless disposition, and easily reclaimed. They are taught to sit on the hand, and a number of them may thus be seen in any Indian bazaar.

# Red-vented Bulbul

± 20 CM, LIGHT FORESTS, GARDENS, HAUNTS OF MAN

CR LC

*Pycnonotus cafer* गुलदुम बुलबुल

The bird, as per historical accounts, is very common all over the district, and is found away from human habitations more often than the Red-whiskered bulbul, which evidently objects to being far from mankind.

One of the best-known birds, the Red-vented bulbul is generally arboreal, with short, weak legs, not adapted to progression on the ground. But the bird sometimes descends to the ground to pick up food. It keeps to the middle levels of trees and bushes, is pleasantly noisy and cheerful, and enjoys dust-bathing. It is commonly found in compounds of large bungalows here.

- Common Tailorbird
- Yellow-bellied Prinia
- Ashy Prinia
- Plain Prinia
- Jungle Prinia
- Graceful Prinia
- Zitting Cisticola
- Grey-breasted Prinia

# CISTICOLIDAE (Tailorbirds, Prinias, Cisticolas)

This is another large family of birds, mostly small in size. They have a drab, brown or grey appearance. They are found in a variety of habitats, such as open country grasslands, scrubs, reeds and open thin forests. Some of the birds in the family have been well adapted as garden birds. Locating these birds in the field, through their call or song, is fairly easier than waiting for a sighting. Being insectivorous, they play an important role as effective pest controllers.

# Common Tailorbird

*Orthotomus sutorius* सामान्य दरजिन

± 12 CM, GARDENS, OPEN FORESTS WITH BUSHES AND CULTIVATION EDGES

CR LC

The Common tailorbird is one of the best-known, small garden birds of the plains. It gets its name from its nest-making skills. A ubiquitous inhabitant of parks, gardens and wooded areas, it is usually seen in pairs. It is very active when foraging and hopping into vegetation searching for insects, and continuously flicks its tail, often erect. Rather common amidst habitations, the Common tailorbird keeps to bushes and shrubs in the gardens. Its nest, mainly built by the female bird in a broadleaved small tree or a low bush, is an example of craftsmanship. The male bird helps in collecting the required material. The nest is placed at an elevated location, either in low bushes, in the hanging boughs of loquat and similar trees, or high up in some lordly mango tree. It feeds mainly on insects but also consumes small fruits, berries, seeds and often nectar.

## Plain Prinia

*Prinia inornata* सादादुम फुदकी

This little bird with a long tail is common in cultivated lands and is similar to many small warblers. It has an olive-brown with pale yellow supercilium with the lower plumage dull greyish. This quaint little bird is one of the commonest of Indian resident birds. It is particularly a bird of standing crops, such as sugar-cane, wheat, millet and the like. It is also partial to long grass in bushes and low-lying cover. It is not very common in Lucknow.

± 13 CM, TALL CROPS, REEDS AND GRASS, ALSO GRASSLAND

CR LC

## Zitting Cisticola

*Cisticola juncidis* जिटजिटी जिटफुदकी

Also known as the Fantail warbler, the Zitting cisticola is a minute, streaked, black-and-brown bird, with pale underparts. It is typically a bird of low, thick cover in wide-open spaces, and is therefore found in stretches of grassland, in patches of reeds or the raised grassy bunds of rice cultivation. When disturbed, the bird jerks itself high into the air, and after flying some distance, falls headlong again into cover.

± 10 CM, OPEN FORESTS, BUSHES, GRASSLAND AND CULTIVATION

CR LC

# Ashy Prinia

± 13 CM, GARDEN, OPEN FOREST WITH BUSHES AND UNDERGROWTH

CR LC

*Prinia socialis* स्लेटीदुम फुदकी

The Ashy prinia is a small, fidgety bird with ashy-grey plumage and a very long tail. This bird is perhaps the most commonly seen and heard bird in the city. Undergrowth or reedy areas alongside waterbodies are ideal sites where the bird can be seen actively moving from bush to bush or a stalk, erecting and flicking its tail. It often sings from a higher perch, such as wires. It usually lives singly or in pairs, and it can be quite bold and fearless. It is an all-season bird of Lucknow.

# ZOSTEROPIDAE

## Oriental White-eye

*Zosterops palpebrosus* पूर्वी बबूना

The Oriental white-eye is a smart, cute, small bird, almost two-thirds of the size of the House sparrow. It is a common bird, often seen in gardens. The bird is named after the ring of white feathers around the eyes. This very active bird is found in mango groves, avenues or compounds, in small parties, diligently searching for nectar and insects. It is a purely arboreal species, which practically never descends to the ground. The white-eye is a sociable bird, always calling and moving about in flocks, in trees, looking out for grubs and fruits. It has a high metabolic rate and feeds all the time.

± 10 CM, GARDENS, OPEN BROADLEAVED FORESTS, ORCHARDS AND MANGO GROVES

CR | LC

- Lesser Whitethroat
- Booted Warbler
- Common Chiffchaff
- Dusky Warbler
- Yellow-browed Warbler
- Tickell's Leaf Warbler
- Greenish Warbler
- Brook's Leaf Warbler
- Hume's Leaf Warbler
- Moustached Warbler
- Clamorous Reed Warbler
- Sulphur-bellied Warbler
- Blyth's Reed Warbler
- Blyth's Leaf Warbler
- Bristled Grassbird
- Striated Grassbird
- Tytler's Leaf Warbler

# SYLVIIDAE (Warblers)

Warblers are perching birds, mostly brown or pale green in colour. Their slender bills are adapted for gleaning insects from foliage. Their nests vary from simple cups to domed structures placed on trees, bushes or grass. Owing to their small size and habits, they tend to be more heard than seen. They inhabit gardens and woodlands. Most of the warblers are passing migrants, and reported in Lucknow at the onset of winter and again before summer. In winter, it is a bird of thick cover, found in any type of habitat, other than thick forests. It hops about the stems in search of insects. They are solitary birds but highly abundant. During its passage through northern India, warblers may be found anywhere—garden, orchards, isolated bushes on barren hillsides, and of course, in any patch of thick cover.

# Common Chiffchaff

*Phylloscopus tristis* सामान्य चिपचिप पतफुदकी

± 11 CM, REED BEDS, LIGHT FORESTS, CROPS AND BUSHES

CW | LC

The Common chiffchaff is very small brown bird found in a variety of wooded and scrubby habitats, often near water. They live singly or in small parties. which search for insects up in the trees, in hedges or among various crops. It often flies out from the extremity of a bough to capture an insect on the wing. It is particularly fond of cotton fields, lucerne, tamarisk and acacias. It has a characteristic habit—not shared by most of the other members of the genus—of hunting in reed beds and undergrowth alongside water bodies. These birds are common in Lucknow during winter.

# Lesser Whitethroat

± 13 CM, SCRUBLANDS AND DECIDUOUS WOODLANDS

**LCW** LC

*Sylvia curruca* छोटी टिकटिकी फुदकी

The Lesser whitethroat is found in shrubby habitats, especially dense hedges with thorny bushes and trees. A quiet, shy bird, which creeps about in trees looking for insects and caterpillars, the Lesser whitethroat is particularly partial to acacias. The bird is often located by its scratchy chortling song that ends with a distinctive loud rattle. It prefers all types of country habitats, except deep forests. Its preference for acacia trees results in its stained yellow head as the pollen is of the same colour. The Lesser whitethroat is a winter migrant in Lucknow.

# Clamorous Reed Warbler

*Acrocephalus stentoreus* बड़ी नरकुल फुदकी

± 19 CM, REED BEDS AND BUSHES AROUND WETLANDS

NCW LC

The largest of the warblers, the Clamorous Reed warbler, is normally a bird of dense reed beds, though, it may also be found in any other thick cover over water. The call and alarm note is a harsh 'chack chack'. Its song is very distinctive, never forgotten once heard. It is loud and variable, hard and metallic for the most part but also interspersed with pleasant bars. Its food consists of the various aquatic larvae and insects, small snails and slugs, and aquatic seeds found in such situations.

# Hume's Leaf Warbler

## *Phylloscopus humei* ह्यूम पतफुदकी

A common bird in the Himalayas, Hume's Leaf warbler is a small Leaf warbler which inhabits higher grounds during the breeding season. During this time, it stays in open coniferous forests and shrubby areas, later descends to the foothills and the plains. This bird is not shy, although its arboreal lifestyle and cryptically coloured plumage makes it difficult to observe it. Its calls are variable, sometimes a sparrow-like chirp. It produces two different songs: a repetition of the two-note call and a long, dry, buzzing trill.

© Rajesh Panwar

± 11 CM, FORESTS, SECONDARY GROWTH AND GARDENS

LCW | LC

# Greenish Warbler

## *Phylloscopus trochiloides* हरी पतफुदकी

The Greenish warbler is a small bird which is olive-green above, yellowish-white below, with a pale wing bar and pale streaking around the eyes. A quiet and undemonstrative bird, it spends most of its time in the winter creeping about the foliage of trees collecting insects, and their larvae and eggs. It is a winter visitor.

± 10 CM, WELL-WOODED AREAS AND SECONDARY GROWTH

CW | LC

# TIMALIDAE (Babblers)

Babblers are a diverse group of birds. Many of the species are terrestrial and spend the day looking for insects among leaf litter. They like to live in a community, so at any point of time, one can see about 8 to 10 birds together. In Lucknow, a few species are most common, while some appear seasonally.

- Tawny-bellied Babbler
- Yellow-eyed Babbler
- Common Babbler
- Striated Babbler
- Large Grey Babbler
- Jungle Babbler

# Yellow-eyed Babbler

± 18 CM, TALL GRASS, BUSHES, REEDS AND SMALL

LCR LC

## *Chrysomma sinense* सोनचश्म चरखी

The Yellow-eyed babbler is a pretty, little bird, larger than the sparrow in size. A prominent physical feature is its yellow eye (iris) and orange-yellow eye-rim, distinctive at close range. It is fond of grassy bushes and dhak jungles. This babbler avoids dense forest and wanders about in open country frequenting tall grass, low scrubs and patches of bushes. It is a familiar garden bird. It is fond of rows of tall grass used as thatch, on the stalks of which, when seeding, it settles and searches diligently for insects. It is often seen in parties of six to a dozen member. In Lucknow, Kukrail forest, parks and areas alongside the river Behta are the best spots to find this bird.

# Jungle Babbler

*Turdoides striata* जंगली गौगाई चरखी

± 25 CM, DECIDUOUS FORESTS, CULTIVATION AND GARDENS

CR | LC

A moderate-sized, earthly-brown bird, the Jungle babbler, is found in noisy squeaking parties, usually on or close to the ground. It goes about in little flocks, popularly called 'seven sisters'. The Jungle babbler is a highly gregarious species. Although it immediately flies up into the branches of trees when disturbed, it feeds, for the most part, on the ground, turning over dead leaves industriously for insects, all the while moving with a clumsy, hopping gait. While feeding, it keeps up a constant chatter, which every now and then, grows very loud. It is found commonly in the compound of bungalows or spaces with mixed tree vegetation. It is a widely distributed bird in Lucknow.

# Common Babbler

*Turdoides caudata* डूमरी गौगाई चरखी

± 25 CM, DRY SCRUBLANDS AND CULTIVATION

LCR LC

The Common babbler is strangely not a common bird in Lucknow. A bird of open country, it is one of the most common and familiar species found in a variety of habitats, in cultivated areas and in gardens, amongst waste rocky ravines studded with bushes. It feeds in flocks, scuttling along the ground, like rats, under hedges or through prickly scrubs and thickets, rummaging for insects. Hopping rapidly about with a bouncing gait, with its long tail trailing, it takes refuge in the bushes or grass, under whose shelter it has been feeding, at the slightest indication of danger. Comparatively weak on the wings, it usually relies on its nimble legs.

# Striated Babbler

*Turdoides earlei* गैंगा गौगाई चरखी

± 21 CM, REED BEDS AND TALL GRASS IN WET HABITATS

**LCR** LC

The Striated babbler is the smallest babbler found in Lucknow. It has a conspicuous and distinct appearance because of its yellow bill and finely streaked crown, throat and breast. Its nest is a massive cup made of grasses, leaves and roots, placed among reed, in a small bush or a small tree, usually close to the ground. The bird is not very common in Lucknow.

# Large Grey Babbler

*Turdoides malcolmi* बड़ी गौगाई चरखी

± 28 CM, OPEN DRY SCRUBS AND CULTIVATION

LCR | LC

A typical sandy-brown babbler, the Large Grey babbler is generally found in noisy and squeaky parties. It is particularly a bird of cultivated plains with open fields, and is never found away from trees. It also appears in gardens, both in large towns and small villages. Half of its time is spent on the trees and the other half on the ground, where it turns over dead leaves and inspects low-growing foliage for insects and other small forms of life, that form a major portion of its diet. Seeds and fruits are also eaten by this bird.

- Indian Bushlark
- Bengal Bushlark
- Ashy-crowned Sparrow Lark
- Sand Lark
- Crested Lark
- Oriental Skylark

# ALAUDIDAE (Larks)

Larks are small- to medium-sized birds of open country, usually dull in colour and known for their beautiful songs. Their colour allows them to blend well with the soil and vegetation. They are generally solitary birds, although they gather in flocks, in agricultural fields, to feed. They are omnivorous and forage on the ground. Most larks are ground nesters and build open-cup nests in small, excavated hollows in the ground. Highly territorial, larks defend their nest site using vocal and flight display.

# Ashy-crowned Sparrow Lark

± 12 CM, CULTIVATION AND OPEN DRY SCRUBLANDS

LCR LC

*Eremopterix griseus* स्लेटीसिर दबकचिरी

This quaint little aberrant lark is one of the most widely distributed birds in India. It is only found in open country with minimal trees. It is, strictly speaking, only a species of the plains.

The Ashy-crowned lark prefers waste ground, fallow fields and semi-desert areas, and feeds on the minute seeds that litter the ground. Found in pairs with a strictly defined territory while breeding, it often collects into large flocks at other times. On the ground, its colouration renders it very inconspicuous, making it extremely difficult to spot these birds.

# Crested Lark

± 18 CM, DRY CULTIVATION, SEMI-DESERTS AND DRY, GRASSY AREAS

CR | LC

*Galerida cristata* चोटीदार चन्डूल भरत

A typical sandy-brown lark, the Crested lark is found in open country in northern India. It can be easily distinguished from other birds by the erect tuft of pointed feathers on its head. It is common in the sandy open plains, both in and about cultivated lands. The bird lives and feeds on the ground, and likes, in particular, a neighbourhood of rough country tracks and roads where it finds corn and insects around the droppings of passing animals. It is far from shy and, on the ground, allows one to approach quite close, walking about with its crest erect and merely flying for a short distance when it does rise above. It also settles on bush tops, stumps, wire fences and overhead wires.

- Thick-billed Flowerpecker
- Pale-billed Flowerpecker
- Plain Flowerpecker

# DICAEIDAE (Flowerpeckers)

Flowerpeckers are named after their tendency to peck at flowers with their bills for nectar, seeds and small insects. Birds in this family are very small, dumpy-looking, often brightly coloured with short, usually straight bills and short stubby tails. Flowerpeckers reside in varied habitats and climates—from the sea level up to more than 12,000 feet (3,700 metres) in altitude where little vegetation grows. The birds are found almost everywhere, from rainforests, secondary growth forests, and woodlands to cultivated farmlands and urban areas.

# Thick-billed Flowerpecker

*Dicaeum agile* भीमचोंच फूलचुकी

± 10 CM, WELL WOODED AREA, ORCHARDS, GARDENS

LCR | LC

The Thick-billed flowerpecker is a tiny, dull-looking bird. It is a bird of well-wooded country and has the habit of flying about singly from clump to clump. Unlike the other birds of the family, the Thick-billed flowerpecker does not swallow the fruit entirely. It plucks it off the clump and with its finch-like beak separates the fleshy epicarp from the sticky seed, swallowing the former, and getting rid of the latter by scraping it off on a neighbouring twig with a sweeping side-to-side motion of the head. It eats three or four berries before flying off to another tree for another round of feeding. It also feeds on a variety of other fruits, particularly those of the lantana scrub and the figs of peepal and gular trees. It also relishes the soft and juicy parts of mahua flowers, and also, small spiders.

# Pale-billed Flowerpecker

± 08 CM, ORCHARDS, GARDENS AND OPEN-BROADLEAVED FORESTS

LCR LC

*Dicaeum erythrorhynchos* छोटा फूलचुकी

A tiny, olive bird with pale underparts and a curved beak, which resembles the female sunbird. It is endemic to the Indian subcontinent, where it inhabits any habitat that is not too dry, too wet, or too high. Entirely arboreal, it seems to have regular feeding territories in which it flits throughout the day. The bird is very restless. It flies from tree to tree, often high in the air; from clump to clump; and on the clumps, it hops from one bunch of flowers to another. All the while, it utters an incessant squeak, 'chik-chik-chik'. Its songs include a unique high-pitched trill. When not singing, the bill can help identify the species.

# NECTARINIIDAE (Sunbirds)

Sunbirds are small passerines, often brightly coloured with iridescent plumage, and short, with almost straight, long and markedly decurved bills. The evolution of its long, curved bills is associated with nectar-feeding. Sunbirds feed on nectar from flowers and insects. Besides being useful in helping reduce numerous insects that may harm plants, sunbirds also help pollinate many flowers, which result in a healthy ecosystem.

- Purple Sunbird
- Crimson Sunbird
- Purple-rumped Sunbird

# Purple Sunbird

± 10 CM, GARDEN, OPEN DECIDUOUS FOREST

CR LC

*Cinnyris asiaticus* बैंगनी शकरखोरा

The Purple sunbird is a little gem of a bird whose cheery notes enliven our gardens. It resembles the hummingbird in the sense that it is dependent on flowers for food. This bird feeds on the nectar produced by various flowering shrubs and trees. Not only the nectar but it also feeds on the various small insects—caterpillars, spiders and flies—that the flowers attract, and in return assists in pollination. Its long tongue is almost tubular in structure and is capable of extrusion beyond the beak. The Purple sunbird usually perches on the twigs and stems of a plant, flitting actively from flower to flower and indulging in a variety of gymnastics to reach the desired food; but when need arises, it can hover with rapidly vibrating wings, though, only for a short time. It is an all-season bird in Lucknow, but its calls are heard from March onward, for almost six months, which is its breeding time.

# PASSERIDAE (Sparrows)

Sparrows are among the most familiar of all wild birds. They are small, seed-eating songbirds with stout bills, though, they also consume small insects. Sparrows can also be seen scavenging for food around cities and will happily eat virtually anything in small quantities. They are predominantly birds of open country with scattered trees and light woodlands. The most significant feature is its close association with humans. Originally through feeding in cultivated areas, and then moving into built-up areas, many species of sparrows nest in holes in occupied buildings.

- House Sparrow
- Chestnut-shouldered Petronia or Yellow-throated Sparrow

# House Sparrow

± 15 CM, HUMAN HABITATIONS, CLOSE TO COW/BUFFALO FARMS AND OPEN COUNTRY NEAR THE CITY

**CR** LC

*Passer domesticus* घरेलू गौरैय्या

There can be no bird that is more universally known and recognised than the House sparrow. This widespread bird is a small, brown bird, not bigger than a tennis ball, with black streaks on its back. It has been closely associated with humans and their lifestyle since ages. The male and the female birds are easily distinguishable, not in size, but in colouration. The House sparrow is known to nest in buildings, finding crevices and holes in walls, or at best, using the birdhouses and nest boxes put out by humans in their gardens. It feeds mostly on seeds, but in the breeding season, the adult bird feeds insects to its young.

House Sparrow (Male)

House Sparrow (Female)

# Chestnut-shouldered Petronia

*Gymnoris xanthocollis* लाल कन्धा गौरैय्या

± 13 CM, OPEN COUNTRY AND EDGES OF CULTIVATION

LCR LC

Also known as the Yellow-throated sparrow, this bird is an unmistakable sparrow with its conspicuous chestnut shoulder-patch and a lemon yellow 'thumb impression' on the throat (absent in the female bird). Unlike the House sparrow, it does not establish itself in human dwellings, and rather keeps more to open scrublands and light deciduous forests. It is essentially a tree sparrow and spends most of its time in the upper branches of trees. Besides paddy grains and grass seeds, the bird also relishes moths and other insects, and nectar too.

# MOTACILLIDAE (Pipits and Wagtails)

Pipits are active terrestrial birds that usually spend most of their time on the ground. A few species make use of trees, perching on them and flying to them when disturbed. Low shrubs, rocks and termite nests may also be used as vantage points by these birds. Some species are sedentary, that is, they do not move long distance, while others are long-distance migrants. Like their relatives, wagtails, pipits engage in tail-wagging.

- Richard's Pipit
- Olive-backed Pipit
- Tawny Pipit
- Tree Pipit
- Long-billed Pipit
- Rosy Pipit
- Paddy Field Pipit
- White Wagtail
- White-browed Wagtail
- Citrine Wagtail
- Yellow Wagtail
- Grey Wagtail

# Olive-backed Pipit

*Anthus hodgsoni* हरी पीठ चरचरी

± 15 CM, OPEN FORESTS AND SHADY BANKS OF WETLANDS

LCW LC

The Olive-backed pipit is a small bird with a greenish-brown back and heavily streaked breast and belly. Often seen in loose flocks or in pairs, this bird prefers forested areas more than other pipits. But it also forages in fields and edges of scrublands. It is tolerant of human activity, and is not uncommon in rural areas and city parks. Its song is a beautiful series of warbling trills, whistles and rattles.

# White Wagtail

± 19 CM, PARKS WITH GRASSY AREAS AND OPEN COUNTRY IN THE VICINITY OF WATER

LCW LC

*Motacilla alba* सफ़ेद खंजन

The White wagtail is a small, dainty bird which walks about on the ground. It is a sociable bird, usually moves about in parties which gather into large flocks when it is time for migration, and often associates with other species as well. It spends most of its time foraging on the ground, preferably in damp places or about the margins of waterbodies, into which, it wades freely. It occasionally perches on trees or buildings. Found near habitation and water, it prefers bare areas for feeding, where it can see and pursue its prey. In urban areas, it has adapted to foraging on paved areas, such as car parking. It nests in crevices in stone walls and similar natural and man-made structures. The White wagtail is a winter visitor, or rather, a harbinger of autumn. It is very common in Lucknow and can be spotted in parks, large lawns and on dry catchments of rivers.

# White-browed Wagtail

*Motacilla maderaspatensis* सफ़ेद भौंह खंजन

± 21 CM, RIVERBANKS, POOLS, LAKES AND IRRIGATION BARRAGES

LCR | LC

This bird is also known as the Large Pied wagtail. This species is a resident and the largest of all wagtail species found in the city. This wagtail is mostly solitary, but can sometimes be seen in pairs or family parties, in the neighbourhood of water. It feeds along the edges of waterbodies, searching for insects, with its long tail incessantly wagging up and down as the bird trips along. It perches freely on rocks and buildings, but practically never settles on trees. The flight of this and other wagtails is rather distinctive, jerky, with a ceaseless rise and fall in the air, and a series of undulating curves.

# Grey Wagtail

± 19 CM, SLOW-MOVING STREAMS AND EDGES OF WETLANDS

**LCW** LC

*Motacilla cinerea* स्लेटी खंजन

The Grey wagtail is a slender bird found alongside slow-moving streams.

It is essentially a bird of mountain streams and rivers, which flow with considerable strength through boulder-strewn beds. But in winter, when it migrates to the plains, it is seldom able to discover these conditions and has to be content with tripping about the margins of a variety of tamer waters, and even feeding on roads and other waterless places. It is a solitaty species and does not gather into flocks like the other wagtails. The bird is a winter visitor to Lucknow.

# Yellow Wagtail

*Motacilla flava* पिलकिया खंजन

± 18 CM, DAMP GRASSLANDS AND PARKS WITH GRASSY SLOPES

LCW LC

The Yellow wagtail arrives in the northern plains as soon as monsoon comes to an end, and passes through until about autumn; they start to leave India during spring, completing the migration just before the onset of summer.

The Yellow wagtail is found in mixed flocks and spends its days feeding on the ground in open grassy locations, preferably damp, or about the edges of jheels or in the pastures around waterbodies. The bird feeds on small invertebrates, both aquatic and terrestrial, and seeds. It roosts at night in reed beds and often congregates with various other species of wagtails at suitable places.

# PLOCEIDAE (Weavers)

Very similar in size and shape to the House sparrow, weavers belong to grassy lowlands near water, with tall standing grass and reeds, especially areas with periodic flooding. Their large, conical bill is a conspicuous physical feature. Largely graminivorous, they prefer feeding on seeds of grass, paddy, millets and weeds. Their diet also includes a certain proportion of insects, mostly small beetles and caterpillars. The young are often fed on invertebrates. They are highly gregarious in nature, roosting and nesting communally, and are noted for their elaborate, long woven grass nests hanging from boughs of trees. The fragmented low lying stretches on one side of the Indira Gandhi Canal, with tall grass, reeds and water, constitute a suitable habitat for weaver birds, and is also perfect for those who wish to watch and study them.

- Black-breasted Weaver or Bengal Weaver
- Baya Weaver
- Streaked Weaver

© Neeraj S.

# Baya Weaver

± 15 CM, GRASSLANDS, SCRUBLANDS AND CULTIVATION

CR | LC

## *Ploceus philippinus* सामान्य बया

A widespread resident bird of the plains, the Baya weaver is found in flocks. Most of them are fulvous birds with black streaks on the upper part of its body. It is a bird of cultivated areas where babool trees and palms stand in the midst of grasslands and arable fields, damp and well-watered localities. The Baya weaver is a social and gregarious bird. It forages in flocks for seeds, both on plants and on the ground. The flocks fly in close formation, and occasionally, descend to the ground to indulge in dust bathing. The Baya is best-known for its nest-making. Its nests are often built on thorny acacia or palm trees mainly, and hung over open water. The nests are long, graceful structures of woven grass, retort-shaped, with the mouth of the nest pointing downwards to the ground. These nests hang in groups of ten or a dozen on a tree. A colony of weavers' nests is one of the most familiar and typical of Indian country scenes.

It feeds on seeds of various kinds and does a great deal of damage to certain crops. But like the sparrow, it compensates for this by eliminating caterpillars, grasshoppers and various other insects on which its young are fed.

© Amit Mishra

# Black-breasted Weaver

± 14 CM, SEASONALLY FLOODED GRASSLAND, REEDS AND CULTIVATION

LCR LC

*Ploceus benghalensis* सरबो बया

Also known as the Bengal weaver or the Black-throated weaver, this species is fairly less common as compared to the other members of this family. It inhabits grassy lowlands near water, with tall standing grass and reeds, and especially areas with periodic flooding. It ventures out into cultivated lands and feeds on seeds of grass, rice, wheat and millet. It searches for insects, especially caterpillars, grasshoppers, spiders and small snails to feed the nestlings. Highly gregarious, foraging and roosting in flocks, it often associates with other similar species.

© Amit Mishra

# ESTRILDIDAE (Munias and Avadavats)

This is a family of small birds with short, stout and conical bills. They seem extremely energetic and vibrant, flitting from stock to stock, or through the undergrowth.

Unfortunately, easy food preferences, flocking habits and small size have earned them a place in cages. Keeping them as cage bird is so popular and in-demand that enormous fraudulent practices have boosted the live bird trade. Silverbills are widespread within the city limits, while munias and avadavats are common in the countryside and light forests.

- Scaly-breasted Munia
- Red Avadavat
- Indian Silverbill
- Black-headed or Tricolored Munia

# Scaly-breasted Munia

± 11 CM, HUMAN HABITATIONS, OPEN CULTIVATION AND BUSHES

CR | LC

*Lonchura punctulata* चित्ति मुनिया

The Scaly-breasted munia, also known as the Spotted munia, is a small finch-like bird. It can be easily identified by the white plumage with dark scale markings on the lower side of its body. It is a bird of the open country, where scrub jungle alternates with cultivated tracts, and wherever vegetation is luxuriant. In such places, it is found in flocks which feed largely in low-seeding herbage, and fly to the bushes, when disturbed, in close order like a swarm of bees. It has a curious petulant little note, 'kitty-kitty-kitty'. Fairly tame and familiar, it comes freely into gardens. It mainly eats grass seeds apart from berries and small insects, and occasionally, devours winged termites emerging from the ground. It is quite common and widely distributed in Lucknow.

Scaly-breasted Munia (Male)

Scaly-breasted Munia (Female)

# Red Avadavat

## *Amandava amandava* लाल मुनिया

± 10 CM, WET GRASS AND REEDS, OPEN FORESTS AND BUSHES

**LCR** LC

The Red avadavats are strikingly pretty, small finch-like birds. Historically known for being a cage and aviary bird, the Red avadavat was captured in large numbers for sale. It is chiefly found in well-watered and well-wooded localities, and is very partial to heavy grass jungles and patches of reeds and grass on the outskirts of local lakes. In such localities, it is found in flocks which perch on top of the tall flowering grasses. It is locally found within the campus of the Sanjay Gandhi Post Graduate Institute and low-lying grassy areas alongside the Indira Gandhi Canal.

Red Avadavat (Male)

© Amit Mishra

Red Avadavat (Female)

© Amit Mishra

# Indian Silverbill

*Euodice malabarica* सादा मुनिया

± 11 CM, HUMAN HABITATIONS, GARDENS AND BUSHES

CR | LC

Also known as the White-throated munia, the Indian silverbill is a small, rather elongated brown bird. It is a popular garden bird, where it is found in small parties. Usually tame and dull, it takes to flight in close order when disturbed, uttering a small 'cheet-cheet-cheet' or 'tee-tee' note. The bird lives on small seeds, which it gathers from the ground, though it is very partial to feeding on the heads of grass and crops, like millet. It also feeds on insects and has been known to visit nectar-bearing flowers. It comfortably inhabits and breeds in well-wooded areas.

# Black-headed Munia

*Lonchura malacca* कलसिरी मुनिया

± 11 CM, WET AREAS WITH TALL GRASS AND REEDS

CR | LC

The Black-headed or Tricoloured munia is a small bird of weedy and grassy areas. It is often seen in small flocks, which associate readily with other seedeaters. The adult bird is handsome and striking with rusty upperparts, while the juvenile bird is notably plain, buffy and brown. According to a study, the Tricoloured munia has very long, curved nails that assist them in clinging to swaying grass stems while feeding.

# FRINGILLIDAE (Finches)

Finches are small- to medium-sized birds. They have stout conical bills adapted to eating seeds. They usually prefer well-wooded areas and forage mostly on the ground. They are strong fliers, and are able to hop and run over short distances. Some species migrate over long distances to warmer climates, while others wander constantly in search for food. Primarily granivorous, they also feed on a wide range of food, such as fruits, berries and insects. Their nests are basket-shaped and usually built on trees. Finches are highly gregarious outside the breeding season.

## Common Rosefinch

*Carpodacus erythrinus* सामान्य लालतूती

The Common rosefinch is an attractive bird with a conical bill, and is similar in size to the house sparrow. The bird is found in all types of open country. It is known to visit well-stocked gardens and the neighbouring villages but avoids heavy forests. This finch feeds on wild cherries, mulberries, and a variety of other seeds and fruits; buds and shoots are also eaten by the bird. It is very fond of the watery nectar of the flowers of the coral tree, and particularly frequents this tree when in blossom. The premises of the Raj Bhavan in Uttar Pradesh is one of the few sites where the bird has been seen. It is a winter visitor to Lucknow.

± 15 CM, OPEN FORESTS, GARDENS AND CULTIVATION

**LCW** LC

© KS Sajwan

# EMBERIZIDAE (Buntings)

Buntings are smaal- to medium-sized birds with strong, conspicuous conical bills designed for shelling seeds, usually small grass seeds. The adults also eat insects in summer. Mostly terrestrial, they can be seen in open habitats—with low, scattered vegetation—in small to medium groups, except during the breeding period when they remain in pairs.

- Crested Bunting
- White-capped Bunting
- Chestnut-eared Bunting
- Red-headed Bunting
- Black-headed Bunting
- Grey-necked Bunting

# Crested Bunting

± 16 CM, DRY, ROCKY OR GRASSY HILLSIDE AND COUNTRYSIDE NEAR OPEN CULTIVATION OR TERRACED CULTIVATION

LCR | LC

*Melophus lathami* चोटी पत्थर चिरटा

The Crested bunting is a solitary bird. The male bird possesses conspicuous, striking, glossy black-and-chestnut plumage with a long, pointed crest. It can be found in a variety of habitats like open bush- and rock-covered mountainside, open country and near cultivated lands. The stony ground and low scrub jungles are havens for the bird. It feeds on the ground, at all times of the day, collecting small grass seeds, but perches and sings on the tops of bushes.

It is a local and common bird of Lucknow and can be observed in the outskirts of the city, light forests and cultivated areas. One can find the bird within the campus of the Sanjay Gandhi Post Graduate Institute and the areas adjacent to the Indian Institute of Management.

# LUCKNOW STATE MUSEUM

## Natural History Section: A Treasure House for Every Naturalist

Façade of State Museum, Lucknow

Carefully Preserved Exhibits on Display

*Birds of Lucknow* is an attempt and aimed to target those who admire and solicit birds, and this would never have been accomplished without a mention of the Lucknow State Museum, and specifically, its Natural History section that harbours rare avian collection. Collection of bird specimen here is like a treasure trove as well as a potential resource to understand and rejoice the overview of the birds and their habitat found in the area, in historical times. This archival avian wealth placed Lucknow in a unique proposition.

The idea of establishing the Museum first clicked into the mind of Colonel Sounders Alexis Abott, the then Commissioner of Lucknow Division, North-West and Oudh Province. Through his personal collection of ethnography and natural history, he laid the foundation of Municipal Museum, Lucknow between 1863 to 1883. It was officially known as the Provincial Museum, North-West and Oudh Province, until 1950. Now, it is known as the State Museum, Lucknow.

What makes the State Museum of Lucknow unique and distinctive is the collection of specimen of birds, which is quite rich and diverse, and also comprises some critically endangered and threatened species.

Pink-headed duck (*Rhodonessacaryophyllacea*) is one of the significant specimens of the museum. Other prominent species are: Great Indian bustard (*Ardeotisnigriceps*), Baer's pochard (*Aythyabaeri*), Siberian crane (*Grus leucogeranus*),White-rumped vulture (*Gyps bengalensis*), Indian vulture (*Gyps indicus*), Bengal florican (*Houbaropsisbengalensis*), Red-headed vulture (*Sarcogyps calvus*) and Sociable lapwing (*Vanellusgregarius*).

Ranked as the fourth oldest museum in India, the Lucknow Museum, as it is popularly known, had specimens of 693 species from 83 families of birds. Some of the specimens were collected in 1823. It makes the collection approximately 195 years old. The largest numbers of specimens were collected during 1870–1880, with last submission in the year 1924. It makes this collection one of the oldest collections of Asia. The major part of the avian collection consists of cabinet skin (approximately 75%). Field slips reveal that these specimens were collected from various parts of India. Among them, the major Provinances were Himachal Pradesh, United Province (Uttarakhand and Uttar Pradesh) Kerala,West Bengal, Sikkim, Punjab Province (Haryana and Punjab) and Nepal. In a few specimen slips, the signature of the collector is present. On the basis of that, it is concluded that there are approximately 100 contributors or collectors of the avian collection. Among them, George Reid, AO Hume, CM Inglis, William Davison, James Murray, William Jessi, Eugene Oats, are a few to mention.

George Reid, one of the members of the management committee of the Lucknow Museum, who was in charge of the Natural History Department of that Institution, has done a commendable service towards ornithologists by compiling an accurate catalogue of the specimens of birds displayed in tha Museum, as on the 1 January 1886. Though the collection is but a small one, containing less than 3,000 specimens (representing rather less than 700 species), half of this collection was collected and presented by Mr Reid himself.

The *Catalogue of Birds in the Provincial Museum, Lucknow, North-West and Oudh Province* in the years 1886 and 1889, had been prepared by him. Though he died at an early age of 58, his contributions in the field of ornithology are remarkable. He took his last breath on 16 March 1901 and was buried in Nishatganj graveyard in Lucknow.

**List of 693 Bird Species with Global Status, as per IUCN**

| *S. No.* | *Status According to IUCN List* | *No. of Species* |
|---|---|---|
| 1. | (Critically endangered) CR | 8 |
| 2. | (Endangered) E | 42 |
| 3. | (Near threatened) NT | 10 |
| 4. | (Vulnerable) V | 20 |
| 5. | (Least concern) LC | 568 |
| 6. | NE | 45 |
| Total | | 693 |

*Source:* State Museum, Lucknow

Tomb of George Reid in Nishatganj Graveyard

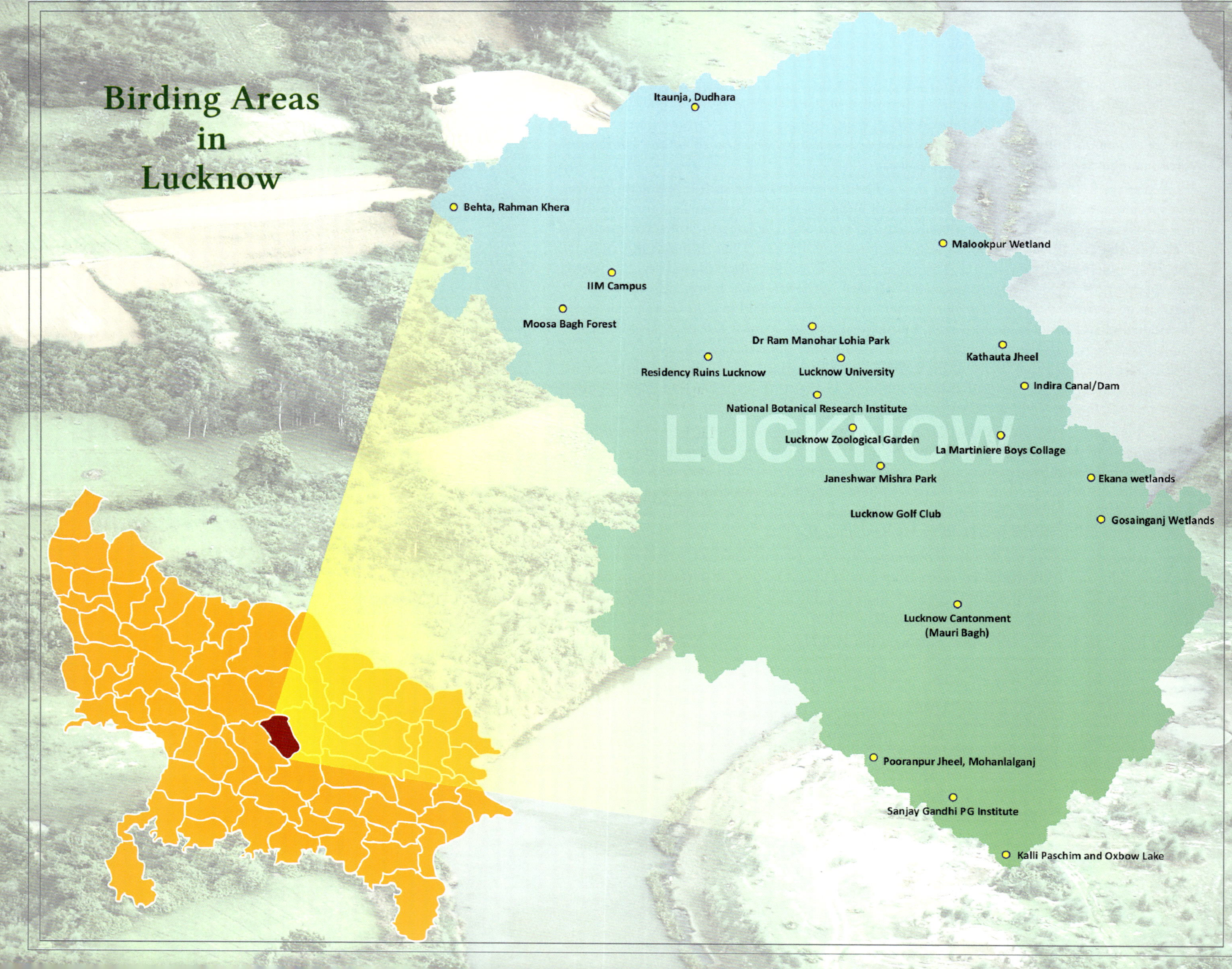
Birding Areas in Lucknow
Itaunja, Dudhara
Behta, Rahman Khera
Malookpur Wetland
IIM Campus
Moosa Bagh Forest
Dr Ram Manohar Lohia Park
Kathauta Jheel
Residency Ruins Lucknow
Lucknow University
Indira Canal/Dam
National Botanical Research Institute
LUCKNOW
Lucknow Zoological Garden
La Martiniere Boys Collage
Janeshwar Mishra Park
Ekana wetlands
Lucknow Golf Club
Gosainganj Wetlands
Lucknow Cantonment (Mauri Bagh)
Pooranpur Jheel, Mohanlalganj
Sanjay Gandhi PG Institute
Kalli Paschim and Oxbow Lake

In the process of evolving a place of its class, Lucknow features wide boulevards, epic monuments, and several parks and gardens that contribute to an atmosphere of faded grandiosity, besides opening an aesthetical side, which is less heard and said. Two major attributes of Lucknow, etiquettes and cuisine, known worldwide, may well be the reason for overshadowing this aspect. A city with imposing monumental structures is an epitome of grace and grandeur, which not only reflects the taste and vision but also depicts the grandeur of the Nawabs living there. Each of the architectural marvels has its own tale to tell. All these heritage structures have one thing in common, plenty of verdant space and lush gardens studded with numerous stout native trees. These tastefully carved insertions add beauty and elegance to the landscape as well as support birdlife and other biodiversity to the full, paving way for birds to nest and roost. This green wealth, in the form of mature and large trees, serves as a nature saviour. One can watch and enjoy the company of hornbills, parakeets, barbets, woodpecker, owls and many other fruit-eating bird species.

City of Lucknow is also acclaimed as the city of gardens. Parks and gardens are woven into the city's landscape since time immemorial. Most of the localities of that time are known as Baghs and each bagh has a story to tell. A few names are Kaiserbagh, Charbagh, Alambagh, Moosa Bagh, Mauribagh, Aishbagh, Vilayti Bagh, Banarasi Bagh, Khurshed Bagh, Sikandar Bagh, Pasand Bagh, and so on. Historical parks served as memorials to historic events or to demonstrate the cultural identity of the clan, while parks created in the modern times were planned more to serve as places for the fun and amusement of the public.

As mentioned earlier in this book, topographically, Lucknow represents the prominent section of the great Gangetic plains and lies almost in the centre of the area between Ganga on the one side, and Ghaghra on the other. Known for productive wetlands, many of these, as per the historical account, were famous for duck shooting. These wetlands are fast disappearing, owing to many reasons, including rampant and unsustainable development. City of Lucknow is now left with only a few of these important ecosystems, mostly in the outskirts. In winter months, these sites transform into vibrant and eventful bird destinations, as migratory birds stay here in large numbers.

River Gomti is an integral part of the city's landscape and said to be the lifeline of the city, traversing from north-west to south-east, supported by the the main tributaries Sai and Behta, and also Kukrail. Catchment and adjoining areas of these riverine system support diversity of birds. Indira Gandhi Canal also forms a potential habitat for birds to breed.

Lucknow Cantonment, proclaimed as one of the largest army areas in the country, possess most precious and potential natural pockets. Owing to its aesthetic character and fairly undisturbed ambience, this area comprises most fascinating bird diversity.

Broadly divided archaeological heritage sites, institutions, old and newly developed parks and natural lakes, all these potential landscapes support both diversity and density of birds, and constitute a vibrant, natural fabric, thereby making the city of Lucknow a well-deserving birding area.

With an evergrowing interest in bird photography, old as well as many new sites have been explored to observe and photograph various bird species. Heritage buildings, surrounded by sumptuous floral diversity and grand old trees, are the favourite sites not only for different species of birds but for bird watchers too. It is estimated that no less than 50 sites in and around Lucknow have become an all-weather retreat and weekend destination for bird watchers.

In this section, we have tried to showcase a few such sites. They form the landscape of the city in the form of parks or garden, historical monuments, institution and wetlands. All these sites share one thing in common, sumptuous green aura to support distinct bird diversity. Among these sites, some are seasonal and some all-weather, but suffice delightfully for those who love and admire nature and birds at large.

| | | |
|---|---|---|
| Behta, Rahman Khera | 26°53'10.5"N | 80°45'57.1"E |
| Dr Ram Manohar Lohia Park | 26°51'17.9"N | 80°58'47.1"E |
| Ekana Wetlands | 26°48'57.3"N | 81°01'04.3"E |
| Gosainganj Wetlands | 26°47'17.7"N | 81°04'58.6"E |
| Indian Institute of Management (IIM) Campus | 26°56'11.9"N | 80°53'58.4"E |
| Indira Canal/Dam | 26°50'03.6"N | 81°04'16.2"E |
| Itaunja, Dudhara | 27°05'26.0"N | 80°50'41.2"E |
| Janeshwar Mishra Park | 26°50'05.6"N | 80°59'19.6"E |
| Kalli Paschim and Oxbow Lake | 26°43'33.5"N | 80°56'15.9"E |
| Kathauta Jheel | 26°51'44.4"N | 81°01'59.8"E |
| La Martiniere Boys College | 26°50'23.7"N | 80°57'45.4"E |
| Lucknow Cantonment (Mauribagh) | 26°49'02.7"N | 80°58'12.5"E |
| Lucknow Golf Club | 26°50'21.1"N | 80°57'27.7"E |
| Lucknow University | 26°51'50.0"N | 80°56'09.0"E |
| Lucknow Zoological Garden | 26°50'43.4"N | 80°57'17.3"E |
| Malookpur Wetlands | 27°04'55.7"N | 80°51'20.1"E |
| Moosa Bagh Forest | 26°52'35.8"N | 80°52'03.2"E |
| National Botanical Research Institute | 26°51'29.5"N | 80°56'59.3"E |
| Pooranpur Jheel, Mohanlalganj | 26°43'34.7"N | 81°00'00.3"E |
| Residency Ruins Lucknow | 26°51'42.4"N | 80°55'33.0"E |
| Sanjay Gandhi PG Institute | 26°45'07.2"N | 80°56'00.5"E |

# Mauribagh, Cantonment

Mauribagh Environmental Park and Training area is spread over 200 acres with 18-holes golf course. Located on Tomb Road (now Kasturba Road), this golf course has been in existence since pre-Independence days. Its exact origin and status remains largely obscure. Set amidst lush green surroundings, this is one such site that harbours sizable bird diversity, which is well recorded in the form of a checklist. A detailed description of the floral and bird diversity is well placed on record in a coffee-table book *Flora and Fauna of Mauri Bagh*. Nearly 200 species of birds, including water birds are reported. A few among the prominent bird species spotted here are: Greater Spotted eagle, Peregrine falcon, Mallard, Jungle Bush quail, Common irora, White-bellied drongo and Mottled Wood owl.

# Sanjay Gandhi Postgraduate Institute and Surroundings

A super-specialty teaching and training medical institute, it is located some 12 kilometres from the main city, on the Lucknow-Raebareli highway. Despite many rounds of makeover and expansion, the sprawling campus still boasts of diversified stretches of green. Lots of forest area, light, dense vegetation and undergrowth, along with man-made water course and tranquil environs, offers plenty of space for a variety of birds, including warblers. Accredited with sightings of prized bird species, like Bristled Grass-bird and Orange-headed thrush, among 200 plus species to its record, SGPGI can be rated as a top-class birding hotspot in Lucknow. Some other prominent sightings here are: Hume's warbler, Sulphur-bellied warbler, Black-winged cuckooshrike, Hair-crested drongo, and Black-headed bunting.

# La Martiniere Boys' College and Adjoining Areas

Though much has changed, which has largely disrupted the link that would otherwise have supported this flourishing biodiversity, it still retains its verdant landscape as well as old-world charm. Nothing illustrates the site better than the vivid description by William Jassie, who did most of his work/observation in and around La Martiniere College.

> **La Martiniere College** stands in a mango-park of about 300 acres. Adjoining this is the Wingfield Park, a large well-kept space filled with trees and ornamental shrubs and renowned amongst the College boys as a place for Bulbuls nests, while further on are the Horticultural Gardens. To the east of the College flows the Goomti, in the banks of which scores of the Indian Sand-Martin and the Bank-Mynah have excavated their holes, and beyond this stretches a level sandy plain dotted here and there with clumps of mango and babool trees. The Oude and Rohilkhand railway crosses the river at right angles, and traverses this plain on its way to Mogul Serai, and all along the sides of the line grow clumps of the tall sharp 'patowal' grass, in which, during the rainy season, the Wren-Warblers weave their beautiful little nests. During the earlier part of the cold weather there is not much to be found near the College. The House-Kite (*Milvus govinda*) breeds in large trees all over cantonments and civil lines, and its nest is a very conspicuous object. One of the most beautiful nests to be found about this time is that of the Thick-billed Flower-pecker (*Piprisoma agile*). It is a beautiful little purse—hanging from a small branch in such a way that the wood makes a sort of rafter as it passes through the nest—and is made chiefly of down and spider's web, mixed with some vegetable fibre, which gives the whole structure a reddish-brown colour. One morning towards the end of March I was walking with some of the College boys through a mango 'top' on the look-out for nests, when we caught sight of a pair of 'Rajah Lals', as the natives call these birds, flying about in the upper branches of one of the biggest mangoes. The mangoes in La Martiniere Park are full of notes, occupied in the earlier part of the season by the Chestnut-bellied Nuthatch (*Sitta castaneiventris*), the Indian Roller (*Coracias indica*), and the Spotted Owlet (*Athene brama*); and later on, in May and June, by the Common Mynah (*Acridolheres tristis*).
>
> From the second week in April to the end of July is the nesting-season, par excellence, in Lucknow. The chief birds then breeding, besides many before mentioned, are the various Cuckoos, Tailor-birds, Warblers, Tree-Pies, Shrikes, Drongos, Crows, Mynahs, Larks, Sparrows, Orioles, and Paddy-birds.
>
> When the 'rains' commence the following may be found breeding—Ground-Cuckoos, Water-birds in general (except Terns), Weaver-birds, and most of the Warblers. Besides these, many of the species already mentioned continue laying. Two species of Ground-Cuckoo occur in Lucknow rarely: the Bengal Sirkeer (*Taccocua Sirkee*) and the common Coucal or 'Crow-Pheasant' (*Centropus rufpennis*). The Sirkeer is a very shy bird and not particularly common.

*Source:* 'Birds Nesting in and around Lucknow'. *The Ibis*, Vol. II, 1896.

# Raj Bhavan

The building of Raj Bhavan is more than 200 years old. The structure was known initially as Kothi Hayat Baksh, designed by Major Claude Martin, who came to India in 1785, with Count Dilaly. Owing to his liking of landscape and architectural planning, he secured a position as the chief planner in the court of then Nawab Asaf-ud-Daula.

The two story palatial building 'Hayat Baksh', which means 'life giving', was erected in the eastern side of the city, surrounded by lush environs. This place was declared, even before the Independence, as the official residence of the Governor of United Provinces of Agra and Awadh, and became known as Raj Bhavan after Independence.

The Raj Bhavan, with the presence of large gardens, old native trees and floral diversity, serves as one of the potential birding sites in the city. As per a bird survey conducted few years ago, 86 bird species were observed within its premises. Some of the prominent bird species found here are: Lesser white-throat, Greenish warbler, Common Rose-finch, Pale-billed flowerpecker, Yellow-eyed babbler, and Small minivet.

# Residency

This monument was built by Nawabs Asaf-ud-Daula and Sadat Ali Khan in the late 1700s. Residency used to be the administrative hub of the British, and later became the home of British commissioner of Awadh. It is famous for being a part of the First War of Independence in 1857. Lucknow was one of the main centres for this siege, and the Residency was the main target. Bullets and cannons razed the place down. And what is left today, still bears the mark of that freedom movement. Despite the main building in ruins, lawns and flowerbeds surrounding it are very well maintained, and serve as one of the main tourist attractions of Lucknow. The site has tall, old trees in good numbers. Several broadleaved trees cover the ground, thereby creating nesting and roosting space for many birds. Some of the important bird species found by bird enthusiasts are Common Hawk cuckoo, Jungle owlet, Spotted owlet, Indian Grey hornbill, Rufous treepie, Little swift, Booted eagle and Thick-billed flowerpecker.

# Begum Hazrat Mahal Park

Built in the memory of Begum Hazrat Mahal, this historical site was earlier known as Old Victoria Park. Situated in the centre of the city, the Begum Hazarat Mahal Park is one of the most spectacular gardens owing to its large trees, especially the colossal Semul, *Bombax ceiba*. During spring, the landscape offers a panoramic view with Semul tree blossoms. And this is unarguably the best time of the year to watch a variety of birds, when the nature's wonder tree attracts a variety of fauna, including birds that feed on nectar from plentyful flowers blooming here. Chestnut-tailed starling, Rosy starling, among other birds, can be seen in groups to take their share of nectar in the spring carnival. Old trees present here serve as the roosting place for bats and the Flying Foxes, while the ancient, stout banyan tree offers nesting and roosting site for many bird species.

# Ekana Wetlands and Banks of Gomti River

Once in the outskirts, this catchment on the right bank of river Gomti is a marshy land with plenty of low vegetation that has turned out to be one of the most vibrant areas to spot different wetland birds together. This area has cluster of pools and low-lying areas with typha and reed cover alongside water bodies, and presence of lofty trees, which has attracted not only migratory ducks and stork forage and roost but also birds of prey that congregate there for hunting, at least in winter. Ekana is a potential biodiversity area within the urban vicinity, and undoubtedly, a spectacular site for those who admire birds in their natural environs. This site has become a growing hotspot for nature photographers. Greater Painted snipe, Common snipe, Eurasian wryneck, Black and Cinnamon bittern, Indian Paradise flycatcher, Ruff, Steppe eagle, Brown shrike, Tickell's Blue flycatcher, Moustached warbler are among the few species spotted by the bird watchers.

# Kukrail Forest

An oasis of greenery in the middle of the city, Kukrail Reserve forest is one of the well-known urban forest reserves under the state forest department. In 1978, Kukrail forest was selected to protect the endangered crocodile species of India.

The Crocodile Breeding Centre at Kukrail came up in the year 1978. This effort marked the beginning of state government's efforts towards conservation of crocodiles at a time when only 300 of them were left. This centre is a prominent site for conservation of gharial and crocodile, by artificially hatching the eggs collected from the various rivers, and releasing the young back into the water when they are old enough to defend themselves. With its natural landscape and a meandering stream, this unique urban forest is home to a variety of resident and migratory birds. With the checklist of more than 120 bird species, Kukrail forest is within the top ten birding hotspots. A few bird species found here are: Grey-headed Canary flycatcher, Orange-headed thrush, Verditer flycatcher, Ashy drongo, Eurasian wryneck, Blue-capped Rock thrush and Olive-backed pipit. Forest wagtail, an uncommon and rare bird species to this area, has been spotted here recently.

# Butler Palace and Lake

Once a lively establishment, this imposing structure was built by Sir Spencer Harcourt Butler, the then deputy commissioner of Awadh, in 1915. The palace served as his official residence. Placed at the centre of the city, the Butler Palace serves as residential area for bureaucrats and other government officials. This site also has a lake on the western side of it. Black-crowned Night heron is an iconic species here. Lofty trees alongside the lake are their favourite nesting places. Besides, owing to its verdant character, this is a popular roosting and nesting site for many bird species. Spotted and Jungle owlets, Coppersmith and Brown-headed barbet, Golden and Black-hooded oriole and other garden bird species can be spotted here round the year.

# Vilayti Bagh

One of the most beautiful gardens of the Nawabi era, the Vilayati Bagh is now under the supervision of ASI. Efforts are being made to restore its flora and landscape to give the garden a colonial look and bring back its lost glory. The Vilayati Bagh cemetery, as it is known now, is located on the banks of river Gomti, and the whole area is surrounded with trees and other vegetation. It is a place where graves of British officers rest. The garden was largely destroyed during the siege of 1857. Built in Awadhi style, the place has two beautiful entrances, the more prominent being the west. The east gate at the other end opens towards the Gomti. Even today, the garden lies in the boughs of great natural beauty, trees standing over the remnants in peaceful grace. With the settings and green environs, this site provides safe refuge to various species of mammals. Water-dependent bird species, such as the Grey-headed Fish eagle is found here along with other bird species, such as Common teal, mallard, Black francolin, Grey-headed woodpecker, Pied (Jacobin) cuckoo, Brown Fish owl and Emerald dove.

# Janeshwar Mishra Park

Spread to an area of 376 acre, Janeshwar Mishra Park is so far the biggest park in Lucknow. Claimed to be the largest public garden in Asia, this park area is aesthetically designed with a variety of tree species, besides two water bodies. Complete landscape offers conducive environment for a variety of birds. Verdant and spacious, this park provides an ideal retreat for birds that feed on grass seeds and insects. With the onset of winter, three to four species of wagtails are a sure sight on the grassy plains and slopes here. The park opened for public in August 2014, and is owned and maintained by the Lucknow Development Authority. Presently, the place has been developed as the most favoured site for morning walkers of all age groups, besides being an ideal place for amusement of general public. Around 100 species have been spotted here by the local bird watchers, so far. Pale-billed flowerpecker, Brown Fish owl, Barn owl, Indian Spotted eagle, Temminck's stint and Bonelli's eagle are among the prominent species observed here.

# Indira Gandhi Canal and Adjoining Areas

Indira Gandhi Canal emerges from the river Ghaghra from Girijapuri and is the main source of water supply to more than 10 districts, including Lucknow. Water from the canal is used with the intention of strengthening the course of the Gomti River, to regulate its flow and help improve the river's water quality. A barrage near Indira Canal's aquaduct has been constructed. Water through this dam reaches Kathauta Jheel (via Sharda Canal), primary source of drinking water for more than 8 lakh homes in trans-Gomti area of Lucknow. Presence of water, reedy vegetation all along the banks of the canal and low lying areas supports rich avifaunal diversity. More than 80 bird species have been observed by the bird watchers of Lucknow, so far.

Besides the presence of Sarus crane in good numbers, Jungle owlet, Blyth's Reed warbler, Yellow-eyed babbler, Black francolin, Pied (Jacobin) cuckoo, Cinnamon bittern, Common woodshrike, Blue-tailed bee-eater and Bengal bushlark are among the prominent bird species spotted here.

# River Behta and Rehmankhera

Situated on the Lucknow-Hardoi route, the bridge on river Behta and a Shiv Mandir was built by Raja Tikait Rai, who was the minister during the reign of Nawab Asaf-ud-Daula (1748–1797). The river, an old bridge and an ancient temple still retain the serenity of the area. It has some undulating patches of forests, flowing stream and resubland, that combine to create a habitat favourable for many species of birds. Scrub areas are good to look for Grey partridge. Sprawling forest of about 250 acre at Rehmankhera serves as an ideal retreat for not only birds but mammals, large animals of prey and even tiger—the famous one that made this forest its temporary home for 108 days. Some of the important bird species located here are: White-bellied drongo, Blue-tailed bee-eater, Black-shouldered kite, Yellow-footed Green pigeon and Greater Racket-tailed drongo.

# NBRI and Sikander Bagh

Established in 1789 as a royal garden by the then Nawab of Oudh, Saadat Ali Khan, the CSIR—National Botanical Research Institute, acquired its present name in the year 1978. Prior to that, it was christened as Government Horticultural Garden and National Botanical Garden. Situated in the middle of the city, this area is the most preferred site for morning walkers. This site is extremely rich in floral and avifaunal diversity. The whole area, including Botanical Garden, is known as Sikander Bagh. Fractions of it are of historical importance and looked after by ASI. Sikandar Bagh, a well-laid garden was built in the year 1847 and used as a cultural retreat for the Nawab's family. It is a very old garden, first maintained by the Department of Science of the Government of Awadh, and later in 1875, under the Department of Agriculture. Due to the presence of variety of fruits and large old trees, this is one of the most preferred sites for garden birds. This is, by far, the best site in Lucknow to cherish the presence of peacock, our national bird. They can be seen on the canopy of large trees as well as on the pathways. They successfully breed here and are present in large numbers. Other prominent bird species located here are Common Hawk cuckoo, shikra, Spotted owlet, Jungle owlet, Indian Grey hornbill, Brown-headed barbet, Alexandrine, Indian Paradise flycatcher, Black-hooded oriole, Tickell's Blue flycatcher, Indian nuthatch, Yellow-footed Green pigeon and Tree pipit.

# CHECKLIST OF LUCKNOW BIRDS

| | |
|---|---|
| ***PHASIANIDAE* Francolins, Quails, Indian Peafowl, Junglefowl** | |
| Black Francolin | *Francolinus francolinus* |
| Grey Francolin | *Francolinus pondicerianus* |
| Common Quail | *Coturnix coturnix* |
| Rain Quail | *Coturnix coromandelica* |
| King Quail | *Coturnix chinensis* |
| Jungle Bush Quail | *Perdicula asiatica* |
| Red Jungle Fowl | *Gallus gallus* |
| Indian Peafowl | *Pavo cristatus* |
| ***TURNICIDAE* Buttonquails** | |
| Small Buttonquail | *Turnix sylvaticus* |
| Yellow-legged Buttonquail | *Turnix tanki* |
| Barred Buttonquail | *Turnix suscitator* |
| ***ANATIDAE* Ducks, Swan and Geese** | |
| Lesser Whistling Duck | *Dendrocygna javanica* |
| Greylag Goose | *Anser anser* |
| Greater White-fronted Goose (H) | *Anser albifrons* |
| Lesser White-fronted Goose (H) | *Anser erythropus* |
| Bar-headed Goose | *Anser indicus* |
| Comb or Knob-billed Duck | *Sarkidiornis melanotos* |
| Ruddy Shelduck | *Tadorna ferruginea* |
| Cotton Pygmy-goose or Cotton Teal | *Nettapus coromandelianus* |
| Gadwall | *Anas strepera* |
| Eurasian Wigeon | *Anas penelope* |
| Mallard | *Anas platyrhynchos* |
| Indian Spot-billed Duck | *Anas poecilorhyncha* |
| Northern Shoveler | *Anas clypeata* |
| Northern Pintail | *Anas acuta* |
| Garganey | *Anas querquedula* |
| Baikal Teal (H) | *Anas formosa* |
| Common Teal | *Anas crecca* |
| Red-crested Pochard | *Netta rufina* |
| Common Pochard | *Aythya ferina* |
| Ferruginous Duck | *Aythya nyroca* |
| Tufted Duck | *Aythya fuligula* |
| Greater Scaup (H) | *Aythya marila* |
| Goosander or Common Merganser (H) | *Mergus merganser* |
| Pink-headed Duck (H) | *Rhodonessa caryophyllacea* |
| Common Goldeneye (H) | *Bucephala clangula* |
| ***PICIDAE* Woodpeckers** | |
| Eurasian Wryneck | *Jynx torquilla* |
| Brown-capped Pygmy Woodpecker | *Dendrocopos nanus* |
| Yellow-crowned Woodpecker | *Dendrocopos mahrattensis* |
| Lesser Yellownape | *Picus chlorolophus* |
| Streak-throated Woodpecker | *Picus xanthopygaeus* |
| Grey-headed Woodpecker | *Picus canus* |
| Himalayan Goldenback/Flameback | *Dinopium shorii* |
| Lesser Goldenback or Black-rumped Flameback | *Dinopium benghalense* |
| White-naped Woodpecker | *Chrysocolaptes festivus* |
| ***CAPITONIDAE* Barbets** | |
| Brown-headed Barbet | *Megalaima zeylanica* |
| Coppersmith Barbet | *Megalaima haemacephala* |
| ***BUCEROTIDAE* Hornbills** | |
| Indian Grey Hornbill | *Ocyceros birostris* |
| Oriental Pied Hornbill | *Anthracoceros albirostris* |
| ***UPUPIDAE* Hoopoe** | |
| Common Hoopoe | *Upupa epops* |
| ***CORACIIDAE* Rollers** | |
| Indian Roller | *Coracias benghalensis* |
| European Roller | *Coracias garrulus* |
| ***ALCEDINIDAE, HALCYONIDAE, CERYLIDAE* Kingfishers** | |
| Stork-billed Kingfisher | *Pelargopsis capensis* |
| White-throated Kingfisher | *Halcyon smyrnensis* |

| | |
|---|---|
| Common Kingfisher | *Alcedo atthis* |
| Pied Kingfisher | *Ceryle rudis* |
| ***MEROPIDAE* Bee-eaters** | |
| Green Bee-eater | *Merops orientalis* |
| Blue-tailed Bee-eater | *Merops philippinus* |
| ***CUCULIDAE* Cuckoos, Malkohas and Coucals** | |
| Pied or Jacobin Cuckoo | *Clamator jacobinus* |
| Chestnut-winged Cuckoo | *Clamator coromandus* |
| Common Hawk Cuckoo | *Hierococcyx varius* |
| Indian Cuckoo | *Cuculus micropterus* |
| Eurasian or Common Cuckoo | *Cuculus canorus* |
| Grey-bellied Cuckoo | *Cacomantis passerines* |
| Asian Koel | *Eudynamys scolopaceus* |
| Sirkeer Malkoha | *Taccocua leschenaultia* |
| Greater Coucal | *Centropus sinensis* |
| Lesser Coucal | *Centropus bengalensis* |
| ***PSITTACIDAE* Parakeets** | |
| Alexandrine Parakeet | *Psittacula eupatria* |
| Rose-ringed Parakeet | *Psittacula krameri* |
| Plum-headed Parakeet | *Psittacula cyanocephala* |
| ***APODIDAE* Swifts** | |
| Asian Palm Swift | *Cypsiurus balasiensis* |
| Little Swift | *Apus affinis* |
| ***TYTONIDAE & STRIGIDAE* Owls** | |
| Barn Owl | *Tyto alba* |
| Indian Scops Owl | *Otus bakkamoena* |
| Oriental Scops Owl | *Otus sunia* |
| Jungle Owlet | *Glaucidium radiatum* |
| Spotted Owlet | *Athene brama* |
| Indian/Rock/Bengal Eagle Owl | *Bubo bengalensis* |
| Dusky Eagle Owl | *Bubo coromandus* |
| Brown Fish Owl | *Ketupa zeylonensis* |
| Mottled Wood Owl | *Strix ocellata* |
| Brown Hawk Owl | *Ninox scutulata* |
| *CAPRIMULGIDAE* Nightjars | |
| Large-tailed Nightjar | *Caprimulgus macrurus* |
| Indian Nightjar | *Caprimulgus asiaticus* |

| | |
|---|---|
| ***COLUMBIDAE* Pigeons and Doves** | |
| Common Pigeon or Rock Dove | *Columba livia* |
| Oriental Turtle Dove | *Streptopelia orientalis* |
| Eurasian Collared Dove | *Streptopelia decaocto* |
| Red Collared Dove | *Streptopelia tranquebarica* |
| Spotted Dove | *Streptopelia chinensis* |
| Laughing Dove | *Streptopelia senegalensis* |
| Yellow-footed Green Pigeon | *Treron phoenicopterus* |
| Orange-breasted Green Pigeon | *Treron bicinctus* |
| Emerald Dove | *Chalcophaps indica* |
| ***GRUIDAE* Cranes** | |
| Common Crane | *Grus grus* |
| Sarus Crane | *Antigone Antigone* |
| Demoiselle Crane | *Grus virgo* |
| ***RALLIDAE* Rails, Crakes and Coots** | |
| Baillon's Crake | *Porzana pusilla* |
| White-breasted Waterhen | *Amaurornis phoenicurus* |
| Brown Crake | *Amaurornis akool* |
| Watercock | *Gallicrex cinerea* |
| Purple Swamphen | *Porphyrio porphyria* |
| Common Moorhen | *Gallinula chloropus* |
| Common or Eurasian Coot | *Fulica atra* |
| ***PTEROCLIDAE* Sandgrouse** | |
| Chestnut-bellied Sandgrouse | *Pterocles exustus* |
| Painted Sandgrouse | *Pterocles indicus* |
| ***SCOLOPACIDAE* Sandpipers, Godwits, Stints, Snipes, Curlews** | |
| Black-tailed Godwit | *Limosa limosa* |
| Whimbrel | *Numenius phaeopus* |
| Common Redshank | *Tringa tetanus* |
| Common Greenshank | *Tringa nebularia* |
| Spotted Redshank | *Tringa erythropus* |
| Marsh Sandpiper | *Tringa stagnatilis* |
| Wood Sandpiper | *Tringa glareola* |
| Green Sandpiper | *Tringa ochropus* |
| Common Sandpiper | *Actitis hypoleucos* |
| Ruff | *Philomachus pugnax* |
| Little Stint | *Calidris minuta* |

| | |
|---|---|
| Temminck's Stint | *Calidris temminckii* |
| Dunlin | *Calidris alpine* |
| Common Snipe | *Gallinago gallinago* |
| Pin-tailed Snipe | *Gallinago stenura* |
| ***ROSTRATULIDAE*** **Painted-snipes** | |
| Greater Painted-snipe | *Rostratula benghalensis* |
| ***JACANIDAE*** **Jacanas** | |
| Pheasant-tailed Jacana | *Hydrophasianus chirurgus* |
| Bronze-winged Jacana | *Metopidius indicus* |
| ***BURHINIDAE*** **Stone-curlew, Stone-plover (Thick-knees)** | |
| Great Thick-knee or Great Stone-curlew | *Esacus recurvirostris* |
| Indian Thick-knee or Indian Stone-curlew | *Burhinus (oedicnemus) indicus* |
| ***RECURVIROSTRIDAE*** **Stilts and Avocets** | |
| Black-winged Stilt | *Himantopus himantopus* |
| Pied Avocet | *Recurvirostra avosetta* |
| ***CHARADRIIDAE*** **Plovers and Lapwings** | |
| Little-ringed Plover | *Charadrius dubius* |
| Kentish Plover | *Charadrius alexandrines* |
| Red-wattled Lapwing | *Vanellus indicus* |
| Yellow-wattled Lapwing | *Vanellus malabaricus* |
| River Lapwing | *Vanellus duvaucelii* |
| Grey-headed Lapwing | *Vanellus cinereus* |
| White-tailed Lapwing | *Vanellus leucurus* |
| ***GLAREOLIDAE*** **Coursers and Pratincoles** | |
| Indian Courser | *Cursorius coromandelicus* |
| Small Pratincole | *Glareola lacteal* |
| ***LARIDAE*** **Gulls** | |
| Brown-headed Gull | *Chroicocephalus brunnicephalus* |
| Black-headed Gull | *Chroicocephalus ridibundus* |
| Caspian Gull | *Larus cachinnans* |
| Pallas's Gull | *Ichthyaetus ichthyaetus* |
| ***STERNIDAE*** **Terns** | |
| Little Tern | *Sternula albifrons* |
| Black-bellied Tern | *Sterna acuticauda* |
| River Tern | *Sterna aurantia* |

| | |
|---|---|
| Whiskered Tern | *Childonias hybrid* |
| ***ACCIPITRIDAE*** **Hawks, Kites, Vultures, Eagles and Buzzards** | |
| Shikra | *Accipiter badius* |
| Indian Spotted Eagle | *Aquila hastate* |
| Greater Spotted Eagle | *Aquila clanga* |
| Oriental Honey Buzzard | *Pernis ptilorhynchus* |
| Tawny Eagle | *Aquila rapax* |
| Imperial Eagle | *Aquila heliacal* |
| Crested Serpent Eagle | *Spilornis cheela* |
| Eurasian Sparrowhawk | *Accipiter nisus* |
| Pallas's Fish Eagle | *Haliaeetus leucoryphus* |
| Steppe Eagle | *Aquila nipalensis* |
| Booted Eagle | *Hieraaetus pennatus* |
| Bonelli's Eagle | *Aquila fasciata* |
| Crested Hawk-eagle | *Nisaetus cirrhatus* |
| White-eyed Buzzard | *Butastur teesa* |
| Short-toed Snake Eagle | *Circaetus gallicus* |
| Long-legged Buzzard | *Buteo rufinus* |
| Eurasian Marsh Harrier | *Cirus aeruginosus* |
| Pallid Harrier | *Circus macrourus* |
| Pied Harrier | *Circus melanoleucos* |
| White-rumped Vulture (H) | *Gyps bengalensis* |
| Indian Vulture (H) | *Gyps indicus* |
| Egyptian Vulture | *Neophron percnopterus* |
| Himalayan Griffon | *Gyps himalayensis* |
| Red-headed Vulture | *Sarcogyps calvus* |
| Black Kite | *Milvus migrans* |
| Black-eared Kite | *Milvus (migrans) lineatus* |
| Black-shouldered/winged Kite | *Elanus caeruleus* |
| ***PANDIONIDAE*** **Osprey** | |
| Osprey | *Pandion haliaetus* |
| **FALCONIDAE** **Falcons** | |
| Common Kestrel | *Falco tinnunculus* |
| Red-necked Falcon | *Falco chicquera* |
| Peregrine Falcon | *Falco peregrinus* |
| Laggar Falcon | *Falco jugger* |

| | |
|---|---|
| ***PODICIPEDIDAE*** **Grebes** | |
| Little Grebe | *Tachybaptus ruficollis* |
| Great Crested Grebe | *Podiceps cristatus* |
| ***ANHINGIDAE*** **Darter** | |
| Oriental Darter | *Anhinga melanogaster* |
| ***PHALACROCORACIDAE*** **Cormorant and Shags** | |
| Great Cormorant | *Phalacrocorax carbo* |
| Indian Shag or Cormorant | *Phalacrocorax fuscicollis* |
| Little Cormorant | *Phalacrocorax niger* |
| ***ARDEIDAE*** **Herons, Egrets, Bitterns** | |
| Indian Pond Heron | *Ardeola grayii* |
| Black-crowned Night Heron | *Nycticorax nycticorax* |
| Grey Heron | *Ardea cinerea* |
| Purple Heron | *Ardea purpurea* |
| Striated Heron | *Butorides striata* |
| Little Egret | *Egretta gazetta* |
| Great Egret | *Casmerodius albus* |
| Intermediate Egret | *Mesophoyx intermedia* |
| Cattle Egret | *Bubulcus ibis* |
| Yellow Bittern | *Ixobrychus sinensis* |
| Cinnamon Bittern | *Ixobrychus cinnamomeus* |
| Black Bittern | *Dupetor flavicollis* |
| ***THRESKIORNITHIDAE*** **Ibis, Spoonbill** | |
| Black-headed Ibis | *Threskiornis melanocephalus* |
| Red-naped Ibis | *Pseudibis popillosa* |
| Glossy Ibis | *Plegadis falcinellus* |
| Eurasian Spoonbill | *Platalea leucorodia* |
| ***CICONIIDAE*** **Storks** | |
| Woolly-necked Stork | *Ciconia episcopus* |
| Painted Stork | *Mycteria leucocephala* |
| Asian Open-bill | *Anastomus oscitans* |
| Lesser Adjutant | *Leptoptilos javanicus* |
| Black-necked Stork | *Ephippiorhynchus asiaticus* |
| ***PITTIDAE*** **Pitta** | |
| Indian Pitta | *Pitta brachyuran* |
| ***CHLOROPSEIDAE*** **Leafbirds** | |
| Golden-fronted Leafbird | *Chloropsis aurifrons* |

| | |
|---|---|
| ***LANIIDAE*** **Shrikes** | |
| Long-tailed Shrike | *Lanius schach* |
| Bay-backed Shrike | *Lanius vittatus* |
| Grey-backed Shrike | *Lanius tephronotus* |
| Rufous-tailed or Isabelline Shrike | *Lanius isabellinus* |
| Brown Shrike | *Lanius cristatus* |
| Southern or Great Grey Shrike | *Lanius meridionalis* |
| ***CORVIDAE*** **Crows, Treepies** | |
| House Crow | *Corvus splendens* |
| Large-billed Crow | *Corvus macrorhynchos* |
| Rufous Treepie | *Dendrocitta vagabunda* |
| ***ORIOLIDAE*** **Orioles** | |
| Indian Golden Oriole | *Oriolus kundoo* |
| Black-hooded Oriole | *Oriolus xanthornus* |
| ***CAMPEPHAGIDAE*** **Minivets, Cuckoo-shrikes** | |
| Small Minivet | *Pericrocotus cinnamomeus* |
| Long-tailed Minivet | *Pericrocotus ethologus* |
| Scarlet Minivet | *Pericrocotus speciosus* |
| Large Cuckooshrike | *Coracina macei* |
| Common Woodshrike | *Tephrodornis pondicerianus* |
| Black-winged Cuckooshrike | *Coracina melaschistos* |
| Black-headed Cuckooshrike | *Coracina melanoptera* |
| Bar-winged Flycatcher Shrike | *Hemipus picatus* |
| ***RHIPIDURIDAE*** **Faintails** | |
| White-throated Fantail | *Rhipidura albicollis* |
| White-browed Fantail | *Rhipidura aureola* |
| ***DICRURIDAE*** **Drongos** | |
| Black Drongo | *Dicrurus macrocercus* |
| Ashy Drongo | *Dicrurus leucophaeus* |
| Greater Racket-tailed Drongo | *Dicrurus paradiseus* |
| Lesser Racket-tailed Drongo | *Dicrurus remifer* |
| Spangled or Hair-crested Drongo | *Dicrurus hottentottus* |
| White-bellied Drongo | *Dicrurus caerulescens* |
| ***MONARCHIDAE*** **Monarchs, Paradise-flycatchers** | |
| Black-naped Monarch | *Hypothymis azurea* |
| Asian Paradise Flycatcher | *Terpsiphone paradise* |

| | |
|---|---|
| ***AEGITHINIDAE* Ioras** | |
| Common Iora | *Aegithina tiphia* |
| Marshall Iora | *Aegithina nigrolutea* |
| ***TURDIDAE* Thrushes** | |
| Blue-capped Rock Thrush | *Monticola cinclorhynchus* |
| Blue Rock Thrush | *Monticola solitaries* |
| Orange-headed Thrush | *Zoothera citrine* |
| Scaly Thrush | *Zoothera dauma* |
| Tickell's Thrush | *Turdus unicolor* |
| Grey-winged Blackbird | *Turdus boulboul* |
| Dark or Black-throated Thrush | *Turdus atrogularis* |
| ***MUSCICAPIDAE* Flycatchers, Chats, Redstarts** | |
| Rufous-gorgeted Flycatcher | *Ficedula strophiata* |
| Red-throated or Red-breasted Flycatcher | *Ficedula parva* |
| Asian Brown Flycatcher | *Muscicapa dauurica* |
| Taiga Flycatcher | *Ficedula albicilla* |
| Tickell's Blue Flycatcher | *Cyornis tickelliae* |
| Little Pied Flycatcher | *Ficedula westermanni* |
| Ultramarine Flycatcher | *Ficedula superciliaris* |
| Blue-throated Flycatcher | *Cyornis rubeculoides* |
| Verditer Flycatcher | *Eumyias thalassinus* |
| Grey-headed Canary Flycatcher | *Culicicapa ceylonensis* |
| Siberian Rubythroat | *Luscinia calliope* |
| White-tailed or Himalayan Rubythroat | *Luscinia pectoralis* |
| Bluethroat | *Luscinia svecica* |
| Oriental Magpie Robin | *Copsychus saularis* |
| Indian Robin | *Saxicoloides fulicatus* |
| Black Redstart | *Phoenicurus ochruros* |
| Common or Siberian Stonechat | *Saxicola torquatus* |
| Pied Bushchat | *Saxicola caprata* |
| Grey Bushchat | *Saxicola ferreus* |
| Brown Rockchat | *Cercomela fusca* |
| ***SITTIDAE* Nuthatches, Wall Creepers** | |
| Indian Nuthatch | *Sitta castanea* |
| ***STURNIDAE* Mynah, Starlings** | |
| Common Mynah | *Acridotheres tristis* |
| Bank Mynah | *Acridotheres ginginianus* |

| | |
|---|---|
| Jungle Mynah | *Acridotheres fuscus* |
| Chestnut-tailed Starling | *Sturnia malabarica* |
| Brahminy Starling | *Sturnia pogodarum* |
| Rosy Starling | *Pastor roseus* |
| Common or European Starling | *Sturnus vulgaris* |
| Asian Pied Starling | *Gracupica contra* |
| ***AEGITHALIDAE* Tits** | |
| Cinereous Tit | *Parus cinereus* |
| ***HIRUNDINIDAE* Swallows, Martins** | |
| Streak-throated Swallow | *Petrochelidon fluvicola* |
| Red-rumped Swallow | *Cecropis daurica* |
| Wire-tailed Swallow | *Hirundo smithii* |
| Barn Swallow | *Hirundo rustica* |
| Plain Martin or Grey-throated Martin | *Riparia paludicola* |
| Dusky Crag Martin | *Ptyonoprogne concolar* |
| Eurasian Crag Martin | *Ptyonoprogne rupestris* |
| Pale Sand Martin | *Riparia diluta* |
| ***PYCNONOTIDAE* Bulbuls** | |
| Red-whiskered Bulbul | *Pycnonotus jocosus* |
| Red-vented Bulbul | *Pycnonotus cafer* |
| ***CISTICOLIDAE* Tailorbirds, Prinias, Cisticolas** | |
| Common Tailorbird | *Orthotomus sutorius* |
| Grey-breasted Prinia | *Prinia hodgsonii* |
| Jungle Prinia | *Prinia sylvatica* |
| Plain Prinia | *Prinia inornata* |
| Ashy Prinia | *Prinia socialis* |
| Yellow-bellied Prinia | *Prinia flaviventris* |
| Graceful Prinia | *Prinia gracilis* |
| Zitting Cisticola | *Cisticola juncidis* |
| ***ZOSTEROPIDAE* White-eye** | |
| Oriental White-eye | *Zosterops palpebrosus* |
| ***SYLVIIDAE* Warblers** | |
| Common Chiffchaff | *Phylloscopus collybita* |
| Lesser Whitethroat | *Sylvia curruca* |
| Dusky Warbler | *Phylloscopus fuscatus* |
| Yellow-browed Warbler | *Phylloscopus inornatus* |
| Tickell's Leaf Warbler | *Phylloscopus affinis* |

| | |
|---|---|
| Brook's Leaf Warbler | *Phylloscopus subviridis* |
| Blyth's Reed Warbler | *Acrocephalus dumetorum* |
| Clamorous Reed Warbler | *Acrocephalus stentoreus* |
| Hume's Leaf Warbler | *Phylloscopus humei* |
| Greenish Warbler | *Phylloscopus trochiloides* |
| Moustached Warbler | *Acrocephalus melanopogon* |
| Booted Warbler | *Iduna calgatai* |
| Sulphur-bellied Warbler | *Phylloscopus griseolus* |
| Blyth's Leaf Warbler | *Phylloscopus reguloides* |
| Bristled Grassbird | *Chaetornis striata* |
| Striated Grassbird | *Megalurus polustris* |
| Tytler's Leaf Warbler | *Phylloscopus tytleri* |
| ***TIMALIDAE*** **Babblers** | |
| Yellow-eyed Babbler | *Chrysomma sinense* |
| Jungle Babbler | *Turdoides striata* |
| Common Babbler | *Turdoides caudate* |
| Straited Babbler | *Turdoides earlei* |
| Tawny-bellied Babbler | *Dumetia hyperythra* |
| Large-grey Babbler | *Turdoides malcolmi* |
| ***ALAUDIDAE*** **Larks** | |
| Ashy-crowned Sparrow Lark | *Eremopterix griseus* |
| Crested Lark | *Galerida cristata* |
| Indian Bushlark | *Mirafra erythroptera* |
| Bengal Bushlark | *Mirafra assamica* |
| Sand Lark | *Calandrella raytal* |
| Oriental Skylark | *Alauda gulgula* |
| ***DICAEIDAE*** **Flowerpeckers** | |
| Thick-billed Flowerpecker | *Dicaeum agile* |
| Pale-billed Flowerpecker | *Dicaeum erythrorhynchos* |
| Plain Flowerpecker | *Dicaeum minullum* |
| ***NECTARINIIDAE*** **Sunbirds** | |
| Purple Sunbird | *Cinnyris asiaticus* |
| Purple-rumped Sunbird | *Leptocoma zeylonica* |
| Crimson Sunbird | *Aethopyga siparaja* |

| | |
|---|---|
| ***PASSERIDAE*** **Sparrows** | |
| House Sparrow | *Passer domesticus* |
| Chestnut-shouldered Petronia | *Gymnoris xanthocollis* |
| ***MOTACILLIDAE*** **Pipits, Wagtails** | |
| Tree Pipit | *Anthus trivialis* |
| Olive-backed Pipit | *Anthus hodgsoni* |
| Paddy field Pipit | *Anthus rufulus* |
| Richard's Pipit | *Anthus richardi* |
| Tawny Pipit | *Anthus campestris* |
| Long-billed Pipit | *Anthus similis* |
| Rosy Pipit | *Anthus roseatus* |
| White Wagtail | *Motacilla alba* |
| White-browed Wagtail | *Motacilla maderaspatensis* |
| Citrine Wagtail | *Motacilla citreola* |
| Grey Wagtail | *Motacilla cinerea* |
| Yellow Wagtail | Motacilla flava |
| ***PLOCEIDAE*** **Weavers** | |
| Baya Weaver | *Ploceus philippinus* |
| Black-breasted Weaver or Bengal Weaver | *Ploceus benghalensis* |
| Streaked Weaver | *Ploceus manyar* |
| ***ESTRILDIDAE*** **Munias, Avadavats, Silverbills** | |
| Indian Silverbill | *Euodice malabarica* |
| Red Avadavat | *Amandava amandava* |
| Scaly-breasted Munia | *Lonchura punctulata* |
| Black-headed Munia | *Lonchura malacca* |
| ***FRINGILLIDAE*** **Finches** | |
| Common Rosefinch | *Carpodacus erythrinus* |
| ***EMBERIZIDAE*** **Buntings** | |
| Crested Bunting | *Melophus lathami* |
| White-capped Bunting | *Emberiza stewarti* |
| Chestnut-eared Bunting | *Emberiza fucata* |
| Red-headed Bunting | *Emberiza bruniceps* |
| Black-headed Bunting | *Emberiza melanocephala* |
| Grey-necked Bunting | *Emberiza buchanani* |

*Note:* The checklist of birds of Lucknow includes bird species with stray occurance as well as historical records.

# PHOTO CREDITS

The photographs in the book have been taken by Sanjay Kumar and Neeraj Srivastava, unless otherwise stated.

Black-winged Stilt

# ACKNOWLEDGEMENTS


We begin with a note of thanks and sincere gratitude towards Dr Asad Rahmani, former director, Bombay Natural History Society, for his unsparing efforts, which enabled us to produce the book in its present pleasing form. It was his vast knowledge of the subject and useful inputs which helped us immensely in fine tuning and shaping the draft of the book. We, once again, thank Dr Rahmani for taking time and kindly writing the forward for the book.

During the entire process of preparation of this book, we came across people who extended their support through knowledge sharing and assistance. We would like to thank them all.

We thank Mr Chander Prakash of Universal Book Sellers, Lucknow, for initiating and coordinating the publication process of the book.

We extend sincere gratitude to Mr Prabhu Narain Singh, the then vice chairman, and Sri Indu Shekhar Singh, chief engineer, both from Lucknow Development Authority, for allowing access to useful information, and to parks and gardens under their jurisdiction, in Lucknow city.

Colonel GK Chaturvedi also offered help and provided valuable inputs on flora and fauna of cantonment of Lucknow.

Our special thanks to Sri AK Singh, director State Museum, Lucknow. Miss Al Saz Fatmi, also from State Museum and in charge of Natural History Section, provided useful and interesting information on specimen of birds collected during the British rule. She deserves a special mention.

Last but not the least, our thanks to Mr Ved Prakash, work-in-charge of Nishatganj Cemetery, for helping us locate and photograph the tomb of George Reid, the erstwhile curator of Lucknow Museum.

This book is largely photo dominated. Undoubtedly, photographs of birds and their habitat add vibrancy and value to the book. Our sincere thanks to Mr Amit Mishra, Mr Clement Francis, Mr Kalol Mukherjee, Mr Kalyan Singh Sajwan, Mr Rajesh Panwar, Mr Sunil Kini and Dr Vivek Banerjee, for contributing excellent photographs towards the book.

# REFERENCES


1. Ali, Salim (2012), *The Book of Indian Birds* (13th edition), Bombay Natural History Society and Oxford University Press.
2. Bainbrigge T, Fletcher & Inglis CM (1936), *Birds of an Indian Garden*.
3. Choudhury, BC & Rahmani AR (2016), *Sarus Crane: A Pictorial Life History*, Bombay Natural History Society.
4. Grewal V, Sen S, Singh S, Devasar N & Bhatia G (2017), *A Pictorial Field Guide to Birds of India, Pakistan, Nepal, Bhutan, Sri Lanka & Bangladesh*.
5. Grimmett Richard, Inskipp Carol & Inskipp Tim (2016), *Birds of the Indian Subcontinent*, Bloomsbury Publishing India Private Limited.
6. Jesse W (1896), 'Birds' Nesting in and around Lucknow', *The Ibis*, Vol. II, pp. 185–198.
7. Jesse W (1897), 'Birds Nesting in and around Lucknow', *The Ibis*, Vol. III, pp. 554–562.
8. Macdonald M (2015), *Birds in My Indian Garden*, Aleph Book Company, New Delhi, India.
9. Manakadan R, Daniel JC & Bhopale N (2012), *Birds of Indian Subcontinent—A Field Guide*.
10. Monga, Sunjoy (2016), *Birds of Mumbai Region*, Yuhina Eco-Media, Mumbai.
11. Nevill HR (1904), *Lucknow, A Gazetteer*, Vol. XXXVII, pp. 1–19, Government Printing Press, Allahabad.
12. Pande Satish (2009), *Latin Names of Indian Birds—Explained*. Bombay Natural History Society and Oxford University Press.
13. Rahmani AR & Mohan Dhananjai (2013), *Threatened Birds of Uttarakhand*, Bombay Natural History Society and Oxford University Press.
14. Rahmani AR, Kumar Sanjay, Srivastav N, Bhargava Rajat & Khan Noor I (2013), *Threatened Birds of Uttar Pradesh*, Bombay Natural History Society and Oxford University Press.
15. Reid, George (1879), 'The Pink-headed Duck near Lucknow', *Stray Feathers*, Vol. VIII, p. 418.
16. Reid, George (1880), 'The Birds of Lucknow Civil Division Part I', *Stray Feathers*, Vol. IX, pp. 491–504.
17. Reid, George (1887), 'The Birds of Lucknow Civil Division Part II', *Stray Feathers*, Vol. X, pp. 1–88.
18. Sharar, Abdul Halim (2000), *Lucknow: The Last Phase of an Oriental Culture*, Oxford University Press.
19. *The Imperial Gazetteer of India*, Vol. I (1907), Clarendon Press, Oxford.
20. मेहरा सत्यप्रकाश, ग्रिमिट रिचर्ड, इंस्किप टिम (2004), उत्तर भारत के पक्षी।

Sarus Cranes giving way to expansion and development of the city